IMMERSION
Bible Studies

ACTS

Praise for IMMERSION

"IMMERSION BIBLE STUDIES is a powerful tool in helping readers to hear God speak through Scripture and to experience a deeper faith as a result."
Adam Hamilton, author of *24 Hours That Changed the World*

"This unique Bible study makes Scripture come alive for students. Through the study, students are invited to move beyond the head into the heart of faith."
Bishop Joseph W. Walker, author of *Love and Intimacy*

"If you're looking for a deeper knowledge and understanding of God's Word, you must dive into IMMERSION BIBLE STUDIES! Whether in a group setting or as an individual, you will experience God and his unconditional love for each of us in a whole new way."
Pete Wilson, founding and senior pastor of Cross Point Church

"This beautiful series helps readers become fluent in the words and thoughts of God, for purposes of illumination, strength building, and developing a closer walk with the One who loves us so."
Laurie Beth Jones, author of *Jesus, CEO* and *The Path*

"I highly commend to you IMMERSION BIBLE STUDIES, which tells us what the Bible teaches and how to apply it personally."
John Ed Mathison, author of *Treasures of the Transformed Life*

"The IMMERSION BIBLE STUDIES series is no less than a game changer. It ignites the purpose and power of Scripture by showing us how to do more than just know God or love God; it gives us the tools to love like God as well."
Shane Stanford, author of *You Can't Do Everything . . . So Do Something*

IMMERSION
Bible Studies

ACTS

Craig S. Keener

Abingdon Press

Nashville

ACTS
IMMERSION BIBLE STUDIES
by Craig S. Keener

Copyright © 2011 by Abingdon Press

Library of Congress Cataloging-in-Publication Data

Keener, Craig S., 1960-
  Acts / by Craig S. Keener.
  p. cm. — (Immersion Bible Studies)
  ISBN 978-1-4267-0985-2 (Curriculum—printed/text plus-cover, adhesive - perfect binding: alk. paper)
  1. Bible. N.T. Acts — Textbooks. I. Title.
  BS2626.K44 2011
  226.6'07—dc22

2010049895

Editor: Mark Price
Leader Guide Writer: John P. "Jack" Gilbert

11 12 13 14 15 16 17 18 19 20—10 9 8 7 6 5 4 3 2 1

Manufactured in the United States of America

Contents

Review Team

Diane Blum
Pastor
East End United Methodist Church
Nashville, Tennessee

Susan Cox
Pastor
McMurry United Methodist Church
Claycomo, Missouri

Margaret Ann Crain
Professor of Christian Education
Garrett-Evangelical Theological Seminary
Evanston, Illinois

Nan Duerling
Curriculum Writer and Editor
Cambridge, Maryland

Paul Escamilla
Pastor and Writer
St. John's United Methodist Church
Austin, Texas

James Hawkins
Pastor and Writer
Smyrna, Delaware

Andrew Johnson
Professor of New Testament
Nazarene Theological Seminary
Kansas City, Missouri

Snehlata Patel
Pastor
Woodrow United Methodist Church
Staten Island, New York

Emerson B. Powery
Professor of New Testament
Messiah College
Grantham, Pennsylvania

Clayton Smith
Pastoral Staff
Church of the Resurrection
Leawood, Kansas

Harold Washington
Professor of Hebrew Bible
Saint Paul School of Theology
Kansas City, Missouri

Carol Wehrheim
Curriculum Writer and Editor
Princeton, New Jersey

IMMERSION BIBLE STUDIES

A fresh new look at the Bible, from beginning to end,
and what it means in your life.

Welcome to IMMERSION!

We've asked some of the leading Bible scholars, teachers, and pastors to help us with a new kind of Bible study. IMMERSION remains true to Scripture but always asks, "Where are you in your life? What do you struggle with? What makes you rejoice?" Then it helps you read the Scriptures to discover their deep, abiding truths. IMMERSION is about God and God's Word, and it is also about you—not just your thoughts, but your feelings and your faith.

In each study you will prayerfully read the Scripture and reflect on it. Then you will engage it in three ways:

Claim Your Story
> Through stories and questions, think about your life, with its struggles and joys.

Enter the Bible Story
> Explore Scripture and consider what God is saying to you.

Live the Story
> Reflect on what you have discovered, and put it into practice in your life.

IMMERSION makes use of an exciting new translation of Scripture, the Common English Bible (CEB). The CEB and IMMERSION BIBLE STUDIES will offer adults:
- the emotional expectation to find the love of God
- the rational expectation to find the knowledge of God
- reliable, genuine, and credible power to transform lives
- clarity of language

Whether you are using the Common English Bible or another translation, IMMERSION BIBLE STUDIES will offer a refreshing plunge into God's Word, your life, and your life with God.

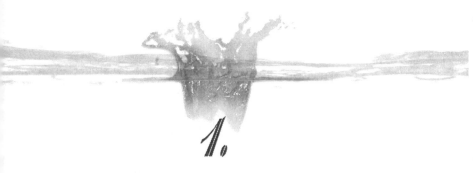

1.

The Power of Pentecost

Acts 1–2

Claim Your Story

Do you ever feel your faith is, well, inadequate—as if Jesus' first followers had access to a dynamic that you don't? Of course, we each have different gifts and backgrounds; some of us are introverts, and some are extroverts, for example. The first disciples also had the advantage of knowing Jesus on a personal level before starting their ministry. Perhaps that fact itself accounts for our feelings of inadequacy.

No doubt the early church experienced a special dynamic. Part of that dynamic was that Jesus' first followers were so sure of their message. The other part was that they were also sure God had given them power. What was so dynamic about the early church was its Holy Spirit-inspired boldness. Luke's narrative about the day of Pentecost and the events leading up to and following it is the story of how God gave them confidence to preach their message by giving them access to the Spirit's power.

Our problem today is not that we lack access to God's power. It is that we often neglect to plug our spiritual appliances into the power source by faith.

Enter the Bible Story

Luke contributed a two-volume work to the Bible: The first volume is an ancient biography about Jesus (the Gospel of Luke); the second is a selective history of the spread of the good news about Jesus to the very heart of the Roman Empire. The first volume begins and ends in Jerusalem; but the second volume, while beginning in Jerusalem, races toward Rome. The first volume grounds us in our Christian heritage; the second volume moves us out into our Christian mission.

At the close of volume one and the opening of volume two, Luke recounts essentially the same scene two different ways, elaborating more details the second time. As the risen Christ was preparing to leave, he promised his followers what they would need in order to carry on his work (Luke 24:36-53; Acts 1:1-11). This pivotal section tells us what was central to Luke and provides the basis for all the rest of the action in the Book of Acts. The church cannot carry out its mission in its own strength; we must believe in the living God and depend on the power that God provides, namely, the Holy Spirit.

Volume two often parallels themes introduced in volume one, so in this case it is helpful for us to remember that it was receiving the Spirit's power in a special way that began Jesus' public ministry (Luke 3:22; 4:18; Acts 10:38). If Jesus, God's Son, depended on the Spirit during his ministry, how much more do we as the church need to do so!

The Promise of Pentecost

According to Luke, in Acts 1:4-8, Jesus ushered in the promise of Pentecost by drawing attention to the priority of the Holy Spirit. Dependence on the Spirit is so important that the Lord did not ask his followers to attempt to begin their mission without it. Of course, with the Spirit comes the power of Pentecost. Jesus promised his disciples power to speak for God like the prophets of old had done. It would be like saying to different people in our Bible study, "You're going to be like Daniel! You will be like Deborah! You will be like Jeremiah!" We often underestimate the power God has given us. Just because we have not plugged in our appliances does not mean that anything is wrong with the power source.

The disciples, however, asked the obvious question (1:6). Jesus had been talking about the Kingdom, and they knew that in Scripture God usually promised the Spirit in the same contexts that promised the restoration of their people. They assumed that Jesus would restore the Kingdom to Israel; but no—he answered instead that some promises remained in the indefinite future, in a time unknown to them. Instead, their task was

The Promised Spirit

This section of Acts is rich in biblical quotations and allusions, particularly about the coming of the Spirit.

Isaiah 32:15; 43:10-12; 44:3, 8; 49:6
In the time of Israel's restoration, the Spirit will make Israel witnesses for God.

Luke 24:44-49; Acts 1:8
The Spirit will make them witnesses for Jesus.

2 Kings 2:9-15
When Elijah ascended, his successor received a special empowerment by the same Spirit.

Acts 1:8-11
When Jesus ascended, he promised empowerment by the same Spirit.

Joel 2:28-29
At the time of Israel's restoration, God will pour out the Spirit on all people.

Acts 2:17-18
At the time of the Messiah's exaltation, God will pour out the Spirit on all people.

Together, these texts suggest how the earliest followers of Jesus understood the promise of the Spirit: an end-time gift, initiating them into a foretaste of the future Kingdom. Further, they had power to bear witness to Christ, just as the prophets of old spoke for God—the difference being that now the ideal was for *all* believers to share this power.

to prepare for that future by being witnesses to the ends of the earth, as God had suggested that Israel would be in the end-time (Isaiah 43:10-12; 44:3, 8; 49:6). Luke often uses the word *power* with reference to signs confirming the message. What shocked the disciples more, however, was the "end-time" mission to the ends of the earth.

Then Jesus ascended to heaven, leaving our dimension, like Elijah of old. As Elijah left the power of the Spirit for his successor, so Jesus charged and empowered the church as his successor.

Preparation for Pentecost

While most of what came next was God's work, Jesus' followers also had something to do. After Luke narrates the promise of Pentecost, he turns to preparation for Pentecost (1:12–2:1), which includes a prayer component

(1:12-14; 2:1) and a political component (1:15-26). Far from sitting idly by, the disciples began praying. Although Luke lets us know that the Spirit came in different ways at different times, prayer fits a common pattern in the coming of the Spirit. Recall the time Jesus was praying and the Spirit came on him (Luke 3:21-22); when the church prayed that its next revival of the Spirit would come (Acts 4:29-31); or when new believers needed an experience of the Spirit and others prayed for them (8:15).

However, the church also had to get its house in order in other respects. In the biggest scandal among those who followed Jesus, one of his closest companions betrayed him. Jesus had appointed 12 disciples to symbolize his plan for the 12 tribes of Israel. If the church was to be ready for God's plan, they needed to make sure the right leaders were in place so they could get down to business as soon as God opened the doors for them. They knew that this leader needed to be someone who knew Jesus' ministry firsthand, and they used their best collective wisdom to narrow the candidates down to two. Once they could not narrow it down any further, they depended on God to narrow it down until they had the right person. Now that they had done or were doing everything they could, it was up to God to fulfill the promise. Their preparation was an act of faith in God's promise.

Many Jews from around the world, along with interested Gentiles, gathered in Jerusalem on the day of Pentecost, the biblical feast of first-fruits. God had planned a strategic moment for pouring out the Spirit. The believers were all together (2:1), presumably continuing in prayer.

The Proofs and Peoples of Pentecost

God offered the proofs of Pentecost, signs that God was acting. People expected the Spirit to come like an end-time wind to bring life to Israel (Ezekiel 37:9-14); and in this case, God sent a powerful wind. John the Baptist had depicted end-time judgment as fire alongside the Spirit (Luke 3:16-17), and so God also sent fire. Most significantly, however (because the scene is repeated on two other occasions—Acts 10:46; 19:6), God enabled Jesus' followers to worship in languages they did not know. What is the significance of that experience? Remember that Luke emphasizes the

About the Scripture

Acts 1: The Call to Be Witnesses

Jesus gave the commission to be witnesses to his eyewitnesses—the apostles and those who were with him (Luke 24:33; Acts 1:2, 21-22). Did Luke record this commission merely to satisfy our historical curiosity, or did he include it to challenge our own witness? Later others became witnesses (Acts 22:15, 20; 26:16). Peter challenges those who behold God's works to recognize that they, too, are witnesses. Moreover, Jesus announced that the Spirit empowers witness (Acts 1:8), yet the Spirit is given to all believers (2:38-39).

Even by the end of Acts 28, the mission was not yet complete. The first apostles, then, were not the only witnesses; they were models for the church's continuing witness.

gift of the Spirit for the purpose of speaking for Christ across all cultural barriers (1:8). What greater symbol of the Spirit's coming on the church could he point to than these early believers worshiping in other people's languages? This gift foreshadows where the entire narrative is headed.

Then Luke introduces us to the peoples of Pentecost (2:5-12). Although these were foreign Jews and converts, not Gentiles, they foreshadowed the mission to all peoples. Luke's list of nations here may recall the first such list in the Bible (Genesis 10), which was immediately followed by the Tower of Babel narrative (Genesis 11:1-9). As God once scattered humanity's languages to divide us at Babel, God also sent the Spirit and an experience of other languages to unite us.

The Prophecy and Preaching of Pentecost

While foreign Jews recognized many of the languages being spoken in 2:4, others mocked the disciples for their apparently ecstatic worship, inviting Peter's explanation from Scripture: the prophecy of Pentecost (2:16-21). Joel had prophesied that God would enable all those in covenant relationship with God to be prophets, regardless of gender, class, or age. (Since at least the 19th century, called women such as African Methodist Episcopal [AME] evangelist Julia Foote have rightly appealed to this passage to support their ministries.) Peter adapted the wording,

---

About the Christian Faith

Dramatic Signs of the Spirit

Although the experience of "speaking in tongues" described in Acts 2:4 is now shared by some people in most denominations, many still think of Pentecostalism when they hear of this experience. The earliest Pentecostals belonged to groups of radical Protestants who were praying that God would give them "missionary tongues" so they could evangelize the world quickly, without having to learn other people's languages. When they experienced speaking in tongues, many immediately left for other countries, expecting to use their newfound gift. Most quickly discovered that while they had a useful prayer language, they still had to learn local languages; and they abandoned the early "missionary tongues" idea. Nevertheless, their early instincts were not completely wrong.

While not every Christian speaks in tongues, Luke mentions this gift from the day of Pentecost to remind us what his vision of the power of the Spirit was all about: the ability to testify for Christ across cultures. In the church, members of all peoples can become one in Christ. As one of the early Pentecostal leaders, William Seymour emphasized that that is one of the greatest miracles of all.

---

using Joel's context to emphasize that this gift signaled a new age ("in the last days"). He also added a new line to reinforce what Joel already said: "And they shall prophesy."

Having then appealed to the witness of the prophecy, Peter continued to preach (2:22-41). The heart of Peter's message is that God raised Jesus from the dead and enthroned him as humanity's rightful Lord. Throughout the rest of Acts, as well, the Spirit-empowered apostolic message continues to narrate Jesus' resurrection and announce that he is Lord. The Spirit, after all, supplies boldness to preach Christ (1:8).

Breaking off Joel's quote with "everyone who calls on the name of the Lord will be saved" (he later picks up Joel's following "as many as the Lord our God invites" in Acts 2:39), Peter explained what it means to call on the Lord's name. The one at God's side is the Risen One. They were eyewitnesses to Jesus as the Risen One and as "Lord." Therefore, the name on which we must call for salvation is Jesus.

Although some Jewish people may have expected Gentiles to enter new lives in Judaism through baptism, Peter summoned his hearers to turn and embrace the Lord's name by baptism. Like John the Baptist in Luke's first volume, Peter recognized that one cannot depend on ancestry or ethnicity for salvation. As the saying today goes, "God has no grandchildren."

The growth rate in Acts 2:41 sounds astonishing, but keep in mind that much larger numbers of converts are reported in many meetings today. The church does not always grow at the same rate in all places and times, but it often begins with spurts in periods of intense commitment. For example, early Methodists in the United States grew from 300 in 1771 to 300,000 some 40 years later!

The Purpose of Pentecost

The Pentecost narrative is ultimately about the Spirit's fruit as well as the Spirit's gifts, about creating a community as well as reaching the world. We could outline the paragraph like this:

♦ People are converted through Peter's message (2:41).
♦ Believers hold Bible studies, share meals, and pray together (2:42).
♦ Believers share possessions (2:44-45).
♦ Believers eat and pray together (2:46-47a).
♦ Believers come together after seeing how Christians live (2:47).

Today people often sit in churches and watch what goes on. The earliest churches, however, were in some ways more like home Bible studies. Equipped with apostolic teaching, believers prayed for one another and shared meals. In their culture, shared meals could create lifelong bonds of loyalty.

Sharing went beyond meals to meeting one another's needs, valuing people more than possessions (2:44-45). This pattern recurred also at the revival (4:32-35) and fit Jesus' radical teaching about what it means to be a disciple: When we belong to Jesus, so does everything we own. Sharing of goods was a necessary sign of repentance and turning to God. This was a crucial emphasis of John Wesley; unfortunately it is not one that is always remembered by all of his modern followers. When our wallets are converted—when we are willing to sacrifice to serve what God cares about most, namely people—our devotion runs deep.

The long-range consequence of this transforming experience of the Spirit was that people were converted not only through the preaching of the gospel, but also through seeing it lived. As Jesus says in John's Gospel, "This is how everyone will know that you are my disciples, when you love each other" (John 13:35). Unless we share Christ with our words, people will not know the message to which our lives invite them. How we as Christians care for one another in person can also be inviting to those with a longing for genuine community and intimacy in a world that is often impersonal or superficial.

The early Christians saw themselves as brothers and sisters. Families, of course, have their problems; but at their best they also have a commitment to work through them and remain faithful to their identity in relationships with one another. Many people yearn to belong to part of a larger or more wholesome family, and this is a gift the church should be able to offer them in Christ.

Live the Story

So far removed as we are from that first century in the life of the church, we easily buy into the "that was then, this is now" perspective, too quickly accepting our presumptions of inadequacy as faithful witnesses for Christ. The world is different now, we say. We are not Peter, we say. Yet Jesus' first followers expressed their radical dependence on God and turned the world upside down in a way well beyond what was possible in their own inborn capacities. How did they do that? By the power of God's Spirit.

In other words, we 21st-century Christians are just as equipped for witness as those first-century Christians were. As evidence of that, the church in many parts of the world today is experiencing exactly the kind of power and dynamism that we read about in these chapters. Why do you think they see more of that power than we often do in our part of the world? Could it be that we simply need to cultivate a deeper dependence on God's Spirit in our lives?

Would you commit right now to pray for a renewing of the Spirit in your life? How might you adjust your perspective on the adequacy of your witness and see the power of the Spirit as something worth seeking? Don't seek in the sense of straining to feel something or get something or persuade God of something. Rather, pursue with intentionality through earnest prayer, confident in God's Pentecost promise to send the Holy Spirit.

2.

Power and Perseverance During Persecution

Acts 3–8

Claim Your Story

By some estimates, tens of thousands of believers die each year around the world because of their faith. How do you feel when you hear stories of Christians killed for their faith? Whatever the actual numbers, persecution and discrimination on account of commitment to Jesus is a common reality in today's world.

Do you ever wonder how you could endure such testing of your faith? The early Christians offer their example to us. If we believe that we have eternal life through trusting Jesus Christ, then no price can be too great to follow him. We may have many life goals and objectives; but if our highest objectives center in Christ, we can make self-sacrifices as needed. According to Acts, Christians who had already lived sacrificially were the ones ready to stand firm when they had to face suffering beyond their control.

Enter the Bible Story

How much is Jesus worth to us? In some parts of the world, persecution makes Jesus' followers count the cost of following him. In Acts 3–8, the believers empowered in the first two chapters stand firmly and act boldly in spite of opposition.

Healing and Preaching (Chapter 3)

The power of Pentecost encountered in our previous session contin-ues in this one. In the final paragraph of Acts 2, Luke summarizes that God continued performing signs (miracles that draw attention to God) through the apostles and that believers were continuing to worship together in the Temple. In 3:1-11, Luke offers a particularly dramatic example of these points. On the way to the Temple for prayer, Peter and John met a beggar unable to walk. They offered him what they had: the power of Jesus' name. In other words, they acted on his delegated author-ity. The apostles had little of their own to depend on, but God's power met the beggar's need and transformed his means of livelihood.

About the Scripture

Peter and Paul in Luke

Luke often selected and edited aspects of his material that highlight connections among major characters. We may illustrate such connections by observing common ele-ments in Luke's first healing narratives for Peter and Paul. Elements of continuity among major characters in Luke's narrative reinforce the same point that we see in Acts 7: It is the same God working through different servants.

Acts 3:1-6	Acts 14:8-10
Unable to walk "from birth" (verse 2)	Unable to walk "from birth" (verse 8)
Peter and John stare intently (verse 4).	Paul stares intently (verse 9).
Leaping and walking (verse 8)	Leaping and walking (verse 10)
Near Temple gates (verse 10)	Near Temple gates (verse 13)
Rejects credit for divine miracle (verse 12)	Rejects credit for divine miracle (verses 14-15)

As in his sermon in the previous chapter, so in Acts 3:12-26, Peter preached about God raising Jesus after he was rejected. He also alluded to biblical passages (Isaiah's "glorified . . . servant"; a prophet like Moses) that fit the pattern of a rejected deliverer, perhaps also foreshadowing the suffering of Jesus' witnesses in this section.

Persecuted for Speaking Truth (Chapters 4–5)

Not everyone is happy when we try to share with them the wonderful gift we have experienced in Jesus. This is not, however, a new problem. While we might expect something as dramatic as a miracle to convince everyone, evidence sometimes also reinforces the hostility of those determined not to believe.

While other Jewish hearers welcomed the apostolic message, the local elite—especially the Sadducees, who were known for denying the Resurrection (Luke 20:27; Acts 4:1-2)—quickly detained them for their commotion in the Temple. Peter pointed out that they were arraigned only for doing something good. The name of Jesus that "healed" the man is also the only name by which all people may be "saved" (4:12, using the same Greek word). Unable to deny the healing, and still sensitive to public opinion, the elite released them with a warning to stop using Jesus' name. The apostles, of course, would not deny the divine truth that they knew firsthand.

The disciples' fortitude offers a model for us. Instead of becoming discouraged by persecution, the church prayed together, recognizing that the opposition of rulers simply fulfilled what they should expect from Scripture. Accustomed to praying the Psalms, here they employed especially the words of Psalm 2. Instead of becoming intimidated because of the official response to the miracle and Peter's boldness, they prayed for more boldness and more signs. As God answered prayer for the Spirit in Acts 1–2, God responded by sending a fresh outpouring of the Spirit so that all the believers began speaking boldly.

As in Acts 2, this experience of the Spirit caused believers to value people more than possessions, so that whenever anyone was in need, others would sell their resources to meet those needs (4:34-35). Because the community's leaders had the greatest overall knowledge of need, they supervised the distribution of resources until the work became too much for them (6:1-4).

Luke does not just summarize the economic impact of the Spirit's work; he offers positive and negative examples of economic commitment. Barnabas, who will figure later in Acts, contributed his resources generously. By contrast, Ananias and Sapphira desired a reputation for whole-hearted commitment without true sincerity. Although most miracles in the Gospels and Acts are encouraging good deeds, God also guarded the community's holiness, even through judgment (Leviticus 10:1-2). As Achan invited judgment by retaining some of what was consecrated to God (Joshua 7:1), so did this couple. Peter prophetically recognized their sin and pronounced judgment, and prospective converts quickly recognized that devotion to God must be taken seriously.

This miracle, along with more pleasant ones noted in Acts 5:12-16, makes the apostolic preaching impossible to ignore. While confronting this popular movement had dangers, leaders of Jerusalem's sociopolitical elite recognized that the risks of ignoring it were too great. Thus they confronted the apostles for continuing to promote the name of a man that the elite executed, undermining the elite's authority.

The conflict previously narrated in Chapter 4 escalated. Presumably the authorities interpreted the apostles' miraculous escape from the public jail the way they interpreted their other signs: cheap magic tricks, sorcery (a common explanation in antiquity), or perhaps popular collusion rather than consider that the apostles might have been more right than their persecutors were. In words reminiscent of Socrates, and in the spirit of the biblical prophets, Peter simply reiterated his previous insistence that they would obey God rather than mortals. They would continue to speak as eyewitnesses of what they knew to be true. The apostles' refusal to be intimidated was a threat to the elite's honor, therefore enraging them.

We should not think that the entire establishment opposed the apostles. In contrast to the Sadducees, the Pharisees—though probably a minority of the local council—affirmed the Resurrection and treated transgressions more gently. Gamaliel, a well-known Pharisee, who was not unlike some other Pharisees in Luke–Acts, defended God's agents here. If the Jesus movement was simply some human revolutionary movement, it would be crushed. However, what if God were in it? Appealing to the education of his colleagues, Gamaliel alluded to a popular Greek story in which a god freed his servants from prison. In that story, the ruler who opposed those servants was therefore "fighting God" (Acts 5:39).

Though released, the apostles were beaten as a further warning. However, they rejoiced that they could suffer for Jesus' name.

About the Scripture

Anti-Judaism and the New Testament

Because later generations of Christians have sometimes used early Christian portrayals of Jerusalem's leaders in an anti-Jewish way, some readers have assumed that the New Testament portrayals themselves are anti-Jewish. This verdict would, however, be premature. Surviving sources such as the Dead Sea Scrolls, Josephus, rabbinic writings, and even the New Testament describe elite priests (like those among the Sanhedrin) as repressing any groups who disagreed with them. Consequently, to describe the problem facing the early church as simply one of Jews versus Christians would not be accurate. At best, what we know is that the Jewish leaders during the New Testament period often repressed dissenting groups like Jesus' followers.

The Bicultural Witnesses (Chapters 6–8)

Apparently, even ideal churches may face problems not only from hostile detractors outside the church, but also from misunderstandings within it. Given ancient culture, widows were among the most vulnerable persons legally, economically, and socially. Jerusalem's social welfare system depended, primarily, on the support of extended family and the support of local synagogues.

Many foreign Jews wished to spend their last days in the holy city of Jerusalem, but this meant that the foreign Jewish synagogues (6:9) had a disproportionate number of widows to support. Not surprisingly, this social problem spilled over into the church; and the foreign Jewish widows complained that their needs were not being met.

In response, the apostles recognized that they needed to delegate some of their ministry to other qualified persons of integrity, just as Moses had done (Exodus 18:21). So they chose seven people with specifically Greek names to supervise the food distribution. Most Judeans (and some foreign Jews) had Semitic names, but their names revealed that the new supervisors belonged to members of the church's minority group. Who would have foreseen that this group would be a primary bridge to the church's future? As members of a minority culture within a larger one, they were bicultural. As Jews who had tasted life abroad, they were the ones with the greatest natural predilection to carry out Jesus' commission.

These minority leaders served in social ministry, but at least some also preached and performed signs. Luke focuses on Stephen, whose message laid the groundwork for what followed, and on Philip. Lacking another way to counter him, Stephen's opponents in a high-status synagogue (of Greek-speaking Jews founded by Jewish Roman citizens) misrepresented him. They charged him with speaking against Moses and the Law and against "this holy place," the Temple.

Stephen answered the charges against him. Grounded in the Law, his speech was obviously not against the Law. His response to the Temple, though, was more ambiguous: God planned for worship "in this place" (Acts 7:7), but God was not localized in any temple. In fact, against some Jewish traditions, God spoke to Abraham in Mesopotamia and exalted Joseph in Egypt. Not only did he speak to Moses at a mountain in the wilderness, but he called it "this holy ground" (7:33). Against Stephen's accusers, it was not a temple that made a place holy, but God's presence. In fact, Stephen pointed out, even when Israel had a place to worship, they sometimes worshiped wrongly. Following his exposition of the Pentateuch with a reading from the prophets, as in good Jewish homilies, Stephen pointed out that God did not need houses built with human hands.

As was also customary in antiquity, Stephen reversed the charges against his accusers. Speeches typically began with a narrative introduction of the history leading up to the present situation, and Stephen placed his predicament in the context of a history of rejected prophets and deliverers. "Our

Making Connections in Biblical History

By discerning a pattern in how God raised up deliverers in Scripture (Luke 24:44-45), Luke expected his readers to recognize the continuity between the way that God (and God's people) acted in the past (Old Testament) and how they acted in his time (New Testament). God often acted through suffering and rejected deliverers. In highlighting narrative connections among various characters in biblical history, Luke did no more than what some earlier biblical authors had done by comparing Joseph and Moses:

Joseph	Moses
Joseph's family sold him into slavery.	Moses' family, who were slaves, rescued him from slavery.
Midianites sold Joseph into Egypt.	Midianites received Moses when he fled Egypt.
Joseph became a "father" to Pharaoh (Genesis 45:8).	Moses became a son to Pharaoh's daughter.
Joseph was suddenly exalted from slave to ruler over Egypt.	Moses suddenly lost his status in Egypt by identifying with slaves.
Joseph made all of Egypt Pharaoh's slaves (Genesis 47:19).	Moses freed slaves, and God broke Pharaoh's power.
Joseph's God delivered Egypt in famine.	Moses' God struck Egypt with plagues.
Joseph, exiled in Egypt, married an Egyptian.	Moses, exiled from Egypt, married a Midianite.
Asenath's father was priest of On.	Zipporah's father was priest of Midian.
The name of Asenath's first son reflected Joseph's sojourn in a foreign land.	The name of Zipporah's first son reflected Moses' sojourn in a foreign land.
God sent Joseph to bring Israel to Egypt.	God sent Moses to bring Israel out of Egypt.
The future deliverer's leadership was initially rejected by his brothers.	The future deliverer's leadership was initially rejected by some of his people.

ancestors" persecuted Joseph, whom God chose to be a deliverer (7:9). They did the same with Moses, protesting, "Who appointed you as our leader and judge?" (7:27). They even rebelled against Moses in the wilderness. Yet Moses declared that God would raise up a prophet like him. In what way would this future prophet be like Moses? From the points Stephen chose to emphasize in Moses' story, one way the prophet would be like Moses was that his people would initially reject him.

Martyred Like Jesus

We noted above that it was customary for the accused to reverse accusations against his accusers. Yet Stephen indicted not only his accusers, but his judges as well. Stephen accused his audience of being the real violators of God's law (7:51-53). If their ancestors rejected deliverers and (as Jewish tradition recognized) the prophets, they had now rejected the climactic deliverer and continued to resist the Holy Spirit, who was now speaking through Stephen.

What followed was more like a mob lynching than the hearings the apostles had experienced. Yet Luke may be suggesting that a trial occurred —except that Stephen's persecutors were the ones on trial. Judges could stand to render their verdict, and witnesses could stand to testify. Here the Son of man at the Father's right hand was not seated (contrast 2:33-34), but standing (7:55-56). Usually, witnesses stripped a condemned person of their clothes. However, Luke narrates that in this case the witnesses stripped their own clothes. Normally, a person condemned to be executed confessed his or her sins; instead, Stephen confessed the sins of the witnesses.

Most importantly, Stephen emulated Jesus. Stephen and Jesus announced the exalted Son of man at their trials. As Jesus committed his spirit to the Father, Stephen committed his spirit to Jesus. Jesus and Stephen prayed for God to forgive those who killed them. Remarkably, not long after Stephen's death, his prayer would be answered involving one of Stephen's most zealous persecutors: Saul. Though unaware that the witnesses were false, and despite his youth, Saul seemed to play a significant role in Stephen's death. Note that the witnesses deposited their clothes at his feet (7:58) as believers had deposited their gifts at the apostles' feet (4:35, 37; 5:2). Little did Saul know that soon he would spearhead the persecution (8:3), and his conversion would one day help end this phase of persecution.

We might suppose that Stephen was foolish to preach the gospel truth so firmly. Yet Stephen's martyrdom had three important consequences. First, his preaching that God was not localized in the Temple laid the groundwork for the Gentile mission carried out by Philip and eventually by Paul and others. Second, the reaction against his preaching scattered the church through persecution. We might think of that scattering as a negative consequence; but Acts reveals that in God's plan, tragedies are not always what they seem. The scattering of the church led to the evangelization of more people, ultimately including even Gentiles. Finally, a seed was sown in the hard heart of one of his persecutors that would soon take root on the road to Damascus.

Live the Story

For eighteen months, my wife was a refugee in her home country. She has often been surprised when people treat her as a heroine for enduring a situation that she did not choose. She simply had to deal with the situation that came to her. The best gauge of how faithful we would be in different circumstances is how faithful we are right now in the circumstances that we experience. Does Jesus, whom we call Lord, mean more to us than our other pursuits? Do we demonstrate that priority in how we live for him?

Spend time thinking over how these Scriptures in Acts might challenge you to be more radical for Christ. How might these stories encourage you to walk more closely with Christ?

Similarly, remember that these earliest believers were willing to suffer because they had one purpose in mind: to bear witness to the gospel and love of Jesus. They might have avoided persecution by keeping their beliefs to themselves, since no one would have known their convictions. Had they done so, however, the Christian faith would have died out in its first generation.

Do we believe in Jesus enough and care about others enough that we want to share his love no matter what others think?

3.

God's Spirit Compels the Church Across Cultural Boundaries

Acts 8–11

Claim Your Story

Are there groups of people that you don't feel comfortable with culturally? How do you think God feels toward these groups of people? Whether or not there are any cultural groups with which you feel uncomfortable, can you imagine what will happen when the comfort zones of Christians in one culture meet God's heart for the people of another culture? Luke provides a telling case study of just such occasions in Acts 8–10.

From Philip reading the scroll of Isaiah to the Ethiopian official, to Saul's call to the Gentiles, to Peter leading the Jerusalem church into the Gentile mission, to the ministry of Greek-speaking Jews in cosmopolitan Antioch, this section of Acts epitomizes a central thrust of the entire book. The Spirit that empowers the church empowers us to cross-racial, ethnic, and cultural boundaries to share the gospel. God's objective is God's own people, wonderfully different but united in Christ, from all peoples.

Enter the Bible Story

Philip in Samaria (8:5-25)

Although Luke focuses on particular prominent figures, it is clear that all believers were eager to spread their message (8:4; 11:19). Those scattered as a result of Saul's persecution took the message with them wherever they went (8:4). Luke now gives us the particular example of Philip.

About the Scripture

The Samaritans

As another biblical writer puts it, normally "Jews and Samaritans didn't associate with each other" (John 4:9). While they often reckoned them better than Gentiles, the Jews condemned as heretical various Samaritan beliefs, such as their consecration of Mount Gerizim instead of Jerusalem and their rejection of prophets and Scripture after Moses. Strict Jews would not fellowship with Samaritans and could never imagine them as sharers in the same faith and mission.

Luke often uses the term *city* loosely. The Samaritan "city" in Acts 8:5 is not likely the ancient city called Samaria, now a pagan city. Rather, it is likely near ancient Shechem or another community.

God not only enabled Philip to cross forbidden cultural boundaries in 8:5-8, but God also gave him the kind of success in this mission that would have shocked his Judean contemporaries. Philip was not, however, the only one who had been having success. Simon, another worker of extraordinary feats, had long held the Samaritans' attention. Yet now Simon recognized that his magic could not genuinely compete with God's power at work in Philip. Ancients usually attributed to magic any acts of apparently superhuman power that they did not believe were divine.

As a bicultural believer, Philip was among those who led the way in fulfilling the cross-cultural mission Jesus announced in 1:8. Philip's results—probably reported by travelers—presumably astonished hearers in Jerusalem. The apostles then followed Philip's lead and ensured that the new believers had the Spirit. So important was the dynamic of the Spirit in the believer's life that Peter and John made this their focus of ministry to the converted Samaritans.

Christians from different denominations differed over how to apply this scene in which the Samaritans received the Spirit after already receiving Philip's message and being baptized. Many viewed the situation as unusual or enigmatic; others viewed it as the model for a second spiritual experience such as confirmation or Spirit baptism. While we cannot resolve such differences here, one point is clear in view of Luke's larger narrative: The Samaritans receiving the Spirit challenged older models of mission. Luke had already articulated that his emphasis regarding the Spirit involved speaking for Christ (1:8; 2:17-18). The fact that these Samaritans were receiving the Spirit made them not simply recipients of Jerusalem's mission but partners in that mission. Now these Spirit-filled Samaritans would also spread the message about Jesus.

Unfortunately, Simon the magician thought that he could buy God's power the way he had once bought magical formulas. Instead Simon received a curse. His approach to gaining power contrasted with that of the Samaritans who received the Spirit by submitting to the apostles' hands and contrasted the values of the apostles themselves, who did not associate spiritual power with money (3:6).

Sometimes our values are wrong. No matter how much our achievements or resources count in other settings, we must receive God's power humbly as God's gift.

Philip and the African Official (8:26-40)

God's leading is sometimes surprising. The work in Samaria was flourishing; God sent Philip out of his way to meet one individual. That individual, however, was a key person who could carry the message back to his own people. Also important for Luke, this man's conversion reflected the crossing of a significant symbolic barrier: He was Queen Candace's treasurer; but for all his devotion to the Jewish faith, he could not be a full convert to Judaism because he was a eunuch.

Although Luke highlights the Cornelius story because that was the public account that reshaped the thinking of the Jerusalem church, Luke learned of this earlier convert, perhaps from Philip himself. The first actual known Gentile convert (not including those who were already full proselytes to Judaism) was from Africa.

God was so eager for this official to hear the gospel that God arranged for him to be reading a passage that Philip and other early Christians applied especially to Jesus (Isaiah 53). (Although Isaiah often called Israel God's "servant," Isaiah also seemed clear that Israel failed in this servant

The Status of Eunuchs in the Bible

Although Luke likes to credit officials with titles, he reiterates five times that this man was a eunuch (a natural condition for a man who worked closely with a queen). Because eunuchs were excluded from the covenant (Deuteronomy 23:1), the majority of scholars view this official as a God-fearer rather than a full Jewish proselyte. What this means is that he was the first Gentile convert. Although eunuchs were excluded from the covenant of Moses' day, the new covenant would not exclude them. In a text that shortly followed the one this official was reading, God promised to make foreigners and eunuchs part of his people (Isaiah 56:3-7). Even centuries before Philip, an African official who was a eunuch proved to be one of Jeremiah's chief allies (Jeremiah 38:7).

mission and that someone or a remnant within Israel had to bring Israel back to God's way.) This event coincided with an angel's instructions and the Spirit's leading (Acts 8:26, 29-30).

Although Luke's main narrative focuses on the empire of which his audience was a part, he preserves what is likely Philip's testimony that the first Gentile Christian was from somewhere else and that God was eager for the gospel to spread there. His contemporaries thought of "Ethiopia" as at the southern ends of the earth. This account, like the gospel reaching Rome in 28:16-31, thus offers a preview of the good news reaching the ends of the earth.

The Nubian Kingdom

Ethiopia was the Greek term for all Africa south of Egypt, not just what came to be called Ethiopia later. This African official was treasurer of the Candace, a title for queens in the Nubian kingdom of Meroë. This kingdom had existed since about 760 B.C., with its capital in Meroë since about the third century B.C. This civilization was well-known in the Mediterranean world, which regularly remarked that its people were black in color. This empire had repelled Caesar's attempts to conquer it but had trade ties with the Mediterranean world. Archaeologists' discoveries of great wealth there demonstrate that the treasurer's role was a significant one. Meroë had its own language and alphabetic script; but as someone who would be involved in trade with Alexandria and other major cities to the north, this educated treasurer was presumably fluent in Greek.

After Philip's mission with the African official was complete, the Spirit carried him elsewhere; and he evangelized the Judean coast before settling in Caesarea, the Roman coastal capital of Judea. In that mission as in Samaria, he was Peter's forerunner, as we shall soon see (9:32–10:24).

Calling Saul to the Gentiles (9:1-31)

Paul's conversion and call was so important to Luke that he included it (from slightly different angles) three times in Acts (9:1-18; 22:3-21; 26:4-18). Whereas the stories of converted Gentiles that precede (8:26-40) and follow (Chapter 10) it involve God reaching out to Gentiles already seeking the God of Israel, this conversion reveals grace by subduing a Jew who wrongly thought he was obeying God.

Letters of recommendation were common in antiquity, and Saul acquired weighty ones. Letters from the high priest suggested Saul's prominence. Perhaps he belonged to a prominent family in addition to his zeal and learning. It appears that the initiative, in any case, was Saul's. Damascus had no actual extradition treaty with Jerusalem's high priest, but the sizeable Jewish community there would respect him and presumably seek to support his request.

However, Saul encountered the risen Lord en route. How one received Jesus' agents showed how one received him (Luke 10:16), so Jesus demanded to know why Saul persecuted him (Acts 9:4). He repeated Saul's name twice, which calls to mind similar stories in Genesis 22:11 (with Abraham) and in Exodus 3:4 (with Moses). Confronted with what seems to be a divine visitation, Saul was forced to begin reassessing his entire view of God, the law he thought he served, and himself. It is not surprising that he eventually concluded (Acts 13:38-39) that God's righteousness comes as a gift of grace rather than from one's own zeal.

Ananias had a separate and confirming vision. Like Peter in the following chapter, Ananias initially resisted what seemed to be shocking instructions. However, he finally complied so that Saul could receive his sight and be filled with the Spirit. Ananias also conveyed Saul's call to the Gentiles (9:15, confirming what Paul heard on the road according to 26:17-18; and again on a later occasion recounted in 22:21). It is Saul's Gentile mission that makes this story so strategic for the point of Acts.

About the Scripture

Patterns and Paul

Various scholars have observed a pattern in Luke's narrative about Saul. Note the similar sequence of events that took place in two different locations as a result of Saul's unexpected conversion and evangelistic zeal.

Event	Acts 9:13-25 (Damascus)	Acts 9:26-30 (Jerusalem)
Reticence to believe Saul	verses 13-14	verse 26
Reassurance	verses 15-16	verse 27
Saul's association with disciples	verse 19b	verse 28a
Saul's bold preaching	verses 20-22	verses 28b-29a
A plot against him	verses 23-24	verse 29b
Paul's escape	verse 25	verse 30

After this, Saul began preaching in Damascus' synagogues, stirring such a backlash that his allies were forced to send him away under cover of night. His preaching in Jerusalem stirred the same reaction, so that the disciples there were also compelled to send Saul away for his own safety.

Converting Cornelius, Converting the Church (9:32–11:18)

Luke now returns to the story of Peter. Like Philip before him, Peter began to evangelize the Judean coast. Luke liked to pair stories about men and women when possible. So here he recounts the healing of Aeneas and the raising of Tabitha; the latter account closely follows the examples of earlier raisings performed through Elijah, Elisha, and Jesus. These signs garnered widespread attention, so that many turned to Christ. Later, Luke focuses in greater detail on another mission for Peter—a significant turning point for the direction of the church.

The story of Cornelius, so significant that Luke recounts it three times (10; 11:5-17; 15:7-9), is not only about the conversion of Cornelius; it is also about the conversion of the Jerusalem church. Angels had been involved in important events such as announcing Jesus' birth, resurrection, and ascension. In this case, an angel appeared to a Gentile. Cornelius was a centurion. Centurions worked their way up through the ranks, commanded about 80 soldiers, and were the backbone of the Roman army. He had roots in Caesarea, with relatives there.

We do not know whether Cornelius was retired or whether he was married (soldiers were not allowed to marry before retirement, though some had unofficial local concubines before that). Whether Cornelius was a Roman citizen (as his name suggests), a Syrian (like most Roman auxiliaries in Caesarea), or both, he functioned as a representative of Rome, where Luke's narrative is ultimately headed. Caesarea's population was divided between Jews and Syrians, with frequent tensions between them.

Some crucial events in Acts were confirmed not merely by single visions but by paired visions. These occurred with Paul's conversion (9:10-16) and that of Cornelius (10:3-16). That Peter was staying with a tanner may have indicated his willingness to forgo convention (tanning was a despised and notoriously malodorous profession). However, nothing had prepared him for a vision inviting him to eat what the Law called unclean (Leviticus 11). God had earlier commanded Ezekiel to eat unclean food, and Peter's protest against it sounds like that of Ezekiel (Ezekiel 4:14). As the Gentiles arrived, the Spirit explained to Peter that the point was that we must not treat as unclean what God has consecrated. Once again the Spirit urged God's servants to cross barriers for evangelism.

Peter began preaching the gospel story about Jesus (a sort of condensed version of Luke's Gospel) to Cornelius and his guests. Peter came to understand that ethnic universality is part of the message: God shows no partiality. Although the emperor claimed to bring peace and rule the world, Peter showed that Jesus is the true bringer of peace and ruler of all, establishing a true multicultural kingdom.

As Peter preached the Resurrection and faith in Jesus, God's Spirit empowered these Gentiles in the same way the Spirit had touched Jews and Samaritans earlier. Circumcision was a sign of the covenant, but God himself offered a sign of deeper reality confirming his acceptance of these Gentiles.

Showing proper hospitality, the Jews lodged their Gentile guests overnight; and the Gentiles in turn showed hospitality to Peter and his companions for a few days. This behavior led to the heart of the Jerusalem church's accusation: "You ate with [Gentiles]!" (Acts 11:3). Keep in mind that eating with sinners was a standard accusation of Pharisees in Luke's Gospel (Luke 5:30; 7:34; 15:2). How easily Jesus' own followers still fall into that same "religious" role!

Peter responded by simply recounting the same story that Luke has already told us: God confirmed in multiple ways acceptance of these uncircumcised Gentiles through paired visions (Acts 11:5-14), the Spirit's voice (11:12), and the Spirit falling on the Gentiles (11:15-17). In view of their experience of the Spirit, the members of the Jerusalem church, though astonished, recognized God's work among the Gentiles.

The Multiethnic Movement in Antioch (11:19-30)

Now Luke returns to the believers scattered abroad after Stephen's martyrdom. In cosmopolitan Antioch, where many proselytes and God-fearers attended synagogues, the Jewish witness gradually blended into reaching Greek-speaking Gentiles as well. Jerusalem sent Barnabas to check on this development; and Barnabas, being full of the Spirit, readily recognized this crossing of barriers as God's work.

He quickly headed north to procure a colleague he knew would be interested. After Saul had been sent away from Jerusalem, he returned to his home city of Tarsus in Cilicia. There Barnabas, who knew of Saul's divine call to the Gentiles, found him to help with the growing Gentile mission in Antioch.

After Paul's arrival, Luke announced that this city was where Jesus' followers first became known as Christians. Probably Gentiles used this title to make fun of them, borrowing a political label (Caesareans were followers of Caesar, Herodians of Herod, for example), Christians became known as those who thought Jesus Christ was a king. Even if the title started in derision and misunderstanding, we who acknowledge Christ as our King are not ashamed to use it.

When prophets came and announced a coming famine, Christians in Antioch decided that they had to serve the needs of the poorer church in Jerusalem. Like Stephen and Philip, Barnabas and Saul engaged in ministry to the needs of the poor before beginning their Gentile mission (11:29-30; 12:24).

Live the Story

If God led the first believers across their comfort zones to share the gospel and then embrace its recipients as equal partners, what does God demand of believers today? Of course, the test comes not only in sharing the gospel. Our efforts at evangelism may well bring people into the church, but what then? Once we become a family in Christ, we have family responsibilities toward one another.

Think about how your church community welcomes and ministers to diverse groups of people: age groups (children, youth, young adults, middle-aged adults, senior adults); various ethnic groups; different economic groups; and groups with special needs. What barriers do you encounter as an individual Christian when trying to reach these groups? What barriers does your congregation encounter when trying to reach these groups?

God interrupted Philip's success in Samaria to send him to one person who could then reach his own people. Consider how you might more effectively share the gospel with words and life through faithful friendships with people who may not have had the privilege of experiencing Christ's love.

4.

Peter, Paul, and Barnabas on the Road

Acts 12–15

Claim Your Story

Have you ever suffered or had to sacrifice for doing the right thing? Have you ever had people misunderstand, misrepresent, or oppose you because of your decisions to do what you felt was right? How have you felt after making the choice that you believed was right? Such experiences may give you a taste of what Peter, Paul, and Barnabas faced as they engaged in their mission for Christ. They experienced divine confirmations along the way, but this did not mean that they did not face hardship. Serving God can prove hard and hopeful.

Enter the Bible Story

At the close of the last section of Acts, the Antioch church sent Barnabas and Saul with an offering to help the Jerusalem church. Luke leaves us in suspense about them until their safe return from Jerusalem at the end of Chapter 12. Now, however, Luke turns to the plight of the Jerusalem church at the hands of Herod Agrippa.

Danger for God's Work (Chapter 12)

From the human vantage point, self-centered political rulers often seem more important than people devoted to God's service. Through prayer and trust, however, God's servants accomplish things in light of eternity that tyrants cannot. In this case, the tyrant who planned to kill Peter died before him.

Herod Agrippa I was one of Gaius Caligula's party buddies in Rome. After Caligula became emperor, he declared Agrippa king of Judea. Nevertheless, he kept him in Rome, much to Agrippa's dismay. After Caligula's death, the next emperor sent Agrippa back to Judea, where he catered to the most conservative interests, wishing to show his loyalty to Judaism. His brief kingship stirred nationalistic Jewish hopes and increased the understandable dissatisfaction with the Roman governors who followed him.

Herod had James, John's brother, executed. (This is not the same James, Jesus' brother, who later led the Jerusalem church. Like *Simon, Mary, Judas,* and other names, *James* was a common name for Jewish people in this period.) Then Herod arrested Peter, wanting to execute him just after Passover, the season when Jesus had been executed. Herod kept Peter well-guarded, with two guards chained to him and two standing guard outside. Miraculously, an angel of the Lord interrupted Peter's amazingly contented sleep to lead him safely out of the prison.

When the angel left him, Peter, presumably detained in Jerusalem's upper city near the Temple, headed for a house in that part of town, the house of John Mark's mother. In contrast to poorer homes in the lower portions of Jerusalem, downwind of the sewers, this house had its own gate and a servant. Rhoda, the servant, is a central character in this narrative. When she heard the knocking, she left Peter at the door in astonishment.

We miss much of the irony in Luke's account. This house was probably in the general neighborhood of the chief priests and other residents, and Peter was left knocking at the door. Luke earlier mentioned that the church was praying for Peter's safety. When he showed up at the prayer meeting, they did not believe it. When Rhoda insisted, they suggested that perhaps his posthumous "angel" had shown up—when ironically it was an angel that delivered Peter. (In their defense, even Peter himself did not take his experience literally at first!) Thankfully, God often answers our prayers beyond our own expectations.

Nevertheless, like the women at Jesus' tomb, Rhoda reported the good news; but she was not initially believed by the more socially powerful characters in the narrative. They called her insane—just as a governor later called Paul insane or people thought the disciples were drunk on the day of Pentecost. Bystanders who supposed that the visitor was simply Peter's ghost were just as misinformed as those who thought Jesus was merely a spirit after his resurrection. (While Jews held different ideas about resurrected bodies, *resurrection* by definition included the body. No one would have persecuted the disciples for simply claiming they had seen a ghost, a claim made by many people of their day.)

Herod, meanwhile, executed the four guards (presumably only their shift—not all four shifts—would be punished). Unwilling to accept the possibility of a miracle, he had to assume them guilty of gross negligence or collusion. Yet Herod, acting as if he were master of others' life and death, would face his own destiny soon enough. He lacked the true respect for God that checks arrogance.

Unlike Peter, who refused Cornelius's veneration in Acts 10, Herod refused to deter Gentiles who wished to worship him. The angel of the Lord, who struck Peter earlier in the narrative to awaken and rescue him, now struck Herod down. That he was eaten by worms was a fitting end for a tyrant (matching similar depictions of tyrants' deaths in antiquity). In the end, God's word, which Herod sought to suppress, kept multiplying.

Leaving Comfort for God's Work (12:25–13:12)

With the return of Barnabas and Saul to Antioch, Luke now returns geographically to the church there. Multicultural Antioch included Greeks, Syrians, and Jews, with significant contacts among these groups. The Antioch church (presumably the local coalition of house churches) included a multicultural leadership team with varied backgrounds, though perhaps all were Jewish: Simeon, nicknamed Niger, "the dark one," possibly suggesting North African ancestry; Lucius, from Cyrene, a North African city composed of long-term North Africans, Greeks, and Jews; Manaen, who was brought up with Herod Antipas, possibly as a high-ranking servant; Barnabas, a Levite; and Saul, a Roman citizen of Tarsus.

Concerted prayer (backed up with fasting) offered the context for the Spirit confirming their call to the Gentiles. Note that the Spirit here confirmed rather than inaugurated their calling. They already knew God's call for them. Remember also that God's guidance here was general. They did not know the specifics until they were actually fulfilling the work.

Because Barnabas was from Cyprus (4:36), this was a natural location for the mission to start. (Cyprus was also a straightforward voyage from Antioch's coastal city of Seleucia.) Paphos, on the other side of the island, was where the governor lived. The conversion of this governor proved a noteworthy mark of success. Luke places a special emphasis on caring for the poor, but he also often notes the conversion and helpfulness of people of rank and status.

Just as Philip had to contend with Simon in Samaria, so Saul and Barnabas had to contend with Elymas Bar-Jesus. When confronting competing forms of spiritual power, missionaries have often resorted to what they call "power encounters": spiritual demonstrations that God's power exceeds that of other powers. For example, Pharaoh's magicians turned rods (possibly serpents in a catatonic state) into serpents; but Aaron's rod devoured them. Missionaries in Christian history such as Columba and Boniface, as well as some missionaries today, are known for such encounters. In this encounter, the opponent Elymas, like Saul earlier, was struck blind for a time.

About the Scripture

Saul and Paul

Roman citizens had three Roman names. *Paul* was a good name for Roman citizens, but we do not know what Paul's other Roman names were. Jewish Roman citizens also typically had another name, often related in meaning or sound with their Roman name. *Saul* sounded enough like *Paul* to serve this purpose. *Saul* was also a natural name for a Benjamite (which Paul's letters inform us he was), since this was the name of a Benjamite king of Israel. Contrary to what some people think, Saul's name was not changed to Paul at this point. He was born with both names, but the conversion of a Roman governor may have offered the point at which Saul realized that use of his Roman name would be advantageous while ministering among Gentiles.

David's Descendant: Jesus

When Paul preached in a synagogue, he highlighted God's biblical promises to David. God promised David that his descendants would rule forever. Although Israel's present subjugation by other empires precluded an earthly Davidic ruler, Jewish people looked forward to the time when God would deliver and restore his people.

Finding in Scripture hints of the resurrection of a Davidic descendant, Paul preached that Jesus, descended from David, fulfilled this expectation. Indeed, as Peter's sermon showed in Acts 2, Jesus had already begun to reign as exalted Lord at God's side.

Ministry and Opposition in Pisidia (13:13-52)

Although Sergius Paullus resided in Cyprus, where he was governor, inscriptions attest his family in the area of southern Asia Minor where Paul and Barnabas traveled next. Many scholars thus think that Sergius Paullus provided their next lead for mission by referring them to contacts there. Such high-level contacts, however, ultimately failed to deter persecution.

Luke's narrative is full of historical details confirmed by archaeology, details not based on common knowledge of his day. In any case, he wouldn't care to invent such a mission in the obscure interior of Asia Minor. Barnabas and Saul understood that sometimes God wants us to start small. The Roman colony of Pisidian Antioch, for example, may have hosted less than 20,000 residents (and less than 6,000 Roman citizens). Although Luke does not elaborate the details, the inland journey from the coast of Asia Minor to Pisidian Antioch could have required as much as six days' journey uphill. (Pisidian Antioch is not related to the earlier Antioch. *Antiochus* was a common royal name, so many cities were named Antioch.)

Once the mission team reached Pisidian Antioch, the synagogue leaders invited Paul to speak as a visiting scholar from the Holy Land. Like a good orator, Paul was rhetorically adaptable. He offered a good synagogue homily here (13:16-41); later preached about the God who gave rain to Lystra, a farming community; quoted Greek poets before a highly educated crowd in Athens; and offered excellent legal defense speeches in Chapters 24–26. Fitting Paul's calling, Paul' speech intrigued the Gentiles, whom he welcomed, though it angered many of his own people.

Further Struggles in the Interior (Chapter 14)

Chased out of Antioch, the disciples followed the main road to another town to the east, Iconium, where reaction was again divided and the apostles risked significant danger. Finally they came to Lystra, a small Roman colony (begun with perhaps a thousand Roman citizens). Most of the people in the outlying areas who heard Paul preaching publicly, via translation into their local language, were farmers.

When a significant public miracle occurred, however, the crowd identified Paul as Hermes (spokesman for the gods) and Barnabas as Zeus (the chief god). An old tale from this region (Phrygia) lamented that the last time these gods had visited the region, people had proved inhospitable, leading to harsh judgment. These Phrygians were determined not to repeat the same mistake! Paul and Barnabas, however (like Peter with Cornelius, and in contrast to the tyrant Herod Agrippa), refused worship. Their hearers had gotten precisely the

About the Christian Faith

Understanding "Faith"

When good historians composed speeches, ideally they liked to get the content as close as possible to the sort of content the speaker would have given. Luke understood that Paul taught justification by faith, that is, that God declares and/or makes a person righteous on account of faith. This message belongs to Paul and Luke's larger theology of trusting God not only for salvation but also for power to serve him and others.

One question for readers today is, What does Paul mean by *faith*? Western thinkers have often relegated faith to the realm of private subjectivity, as opposed to objective, scientific knowledge. Danish philosopher and theologian, Soren Kierkegaard, called faith "a leap into the dark." Yet this is not how the term *faith* is used in our New Testament. Far from being a leap into the dark, faith is an obedient step into the light, an act of genuine belief that shapes our lives.

opposite impression of what the apostles sought to convey. Sometimes people's presuppositions are so strong that they misinterpret our message in light of what they expect to hear, and we must work hard to clarify our meaning.

Ironically, while Paul was preaching the true God of Israel, some of his Jewish detractors treated him like a blasphemer. Pisidian Antioch, though a sister colony of Lystra, was over a hundred miles to its west. Thus Paul's opponents traveled several days to silence him. Paul was stoned and left for dead, an event briefly mentioned in one of his letters; but God was not finished with his ministry, and Paul carried on.

Opposition did not prevent the establishment of a local church; and when Paul and Barnabas returned through all of these towns, they appointed leaders to help guide the young churches they had founded. However, Luke's summary of their message fit what they had demonstrated in their own lives: We enter the Kingdom through sufferings (14:22). Jesus had taught his disciples to expect a period of suffering before the end, just as he himself had endured great suffering before his resurrection. Contrary to what some popular movies and novels suggest today, if we read the New Testament in context, we see that we must be ready to endure suffering for Jesus until he returns.

Struggles Even Among God's People (Chapter 15)

The slow successes of the Gentile mission faced their challenges even in church. In Acts 15, we see a prime example of people of deep conviction embroiled in conflicts, yet seeking earnestly to resolve them with the aid of Scripture. Already practiced in Scripture, circumcision had become an especially prominent mark of Jewish identity since many Jews had given their lives to keep circumcising their sons during the Maccabean era. Yet Paul knew that mandating non-Jewish converts be circumcised on the mission field would create problems for reaching Gentiles for Christ. Paul also believed that the inward reality of the Spirit mattered more than outward circumcision, which merely symbolized the covenant reality effected by the Spirit in the heart.

So after Paul and Barnabas shared "what God had accomplished through their activity" (Acts 15:4), Peter and James, who had stronger conservative credentials with the Jerusalem church, offered more detailed arguments against the requirement of circumcision.

Finally, James offered a compromise solution that satisfied everyone adequately. Although Jewish people believed that circumcision brought Gentiles into the covenant, they usually allowed that other Gentiles could be saved if they observed minimal requirements such as those that James suggested. Some members of the Jerusalem church might have disagreed with Paul as to whether the Spirit made Gentile Christians true converts and children of Abraham, but no one would deny that they were "saved." With this compromise in hand, Paul and Barnabas could counter circumcisionists by appealing to the consensus of the churches: Gentile converts did not have to be circumcised.

Ultimately, Paul and Barnabas had a falling out—ironically in contrast to the peace recently achieved by the church in Jerusalem. Paul, rightly demanding commitment to the mission, did not trust Mark, who abandoned the mission earlier. Barnabas, rightly insisting on compassion (which he had already shown to Paul earlier), wanted to give Mark a second chance. Even though both had good motives, they separated, perhaps providentially creating two mission teams.

Partnership in mission is important, but we must recognize that conflicts will arise along the way. Their partnership might have ended differently, but God did not abandon either team.

Live the Story

How do the models of Peter, Paul, and Barnabas help us to face suffering for Christ? Consider their example and the reasons they were willing to endure what they did. How can their example help us to serve Christ's caring purposes in the world more fully?

Conflicts occur in the church as well as in the outside world. They are inevitable, yet we should do our best to resolve them whenever possible. Unity is important, even to the point of agreeing to disagree on secondary issues. (Because primary issues may be a different story, we must also ask how to determine which issues are central and which are secondary.) How can we work to stay in the conversation with Christians who disagree with us on secondary issues?

5.

New Possibilities and New Perils for Paul

Acts 16–18

Claim Your Story

Have you ever had friends who shared your heart with a common purpose and vision? If so, you can get a sense of the loyalty that Paul and his companions shared with one another over their common mission to share the gospel.

Have you ever observed positive role models that you wanted to imitate? Too often our culture's heroes are those who appear to be strong or intelligent or attractive. Celebrity status always grabs our attention and our admiration, yet we are also drawn to heroes who sacrifice their own advantages and their well-being for others.

In this session, Paul and his companions will sacrifice and endure hardship to bring the good news about eternal life in Jesus Christ to others. In his own letters, Paul invites believers in the churches he founded to imitate him, sometimes after listing his hardships. Consider ways in which we can learn from the example of Paul and his colleagues.

Enter the Bible Story

Gathering a new mission team, Paul and his colleagues continued to share the gospel sacrificially across barriers, meanwhile modeling for their new churches lives of discipleship.

Finding Partners for the Mission (16:1-5)

Paul and Silas revisited the churches that Paul had founded earlier, sharing with them the conclusions of the recent council in Jerusalem. Because many of these churches were in the southern part of the Roman province of Galatia, Paul's later letter to the Galatians gives us reason to suspect that Paul's teaching here did not fully succeed in countering the impact of the circumcision advocates.

Just as Silas had replaced Barnabas as Paul's main partner in ministry, Timothy replaced Barnabas's relative Mark. Yet Paul circumcised Timothy. Why would he do that, especially after refusing to circumcise Gentiles in Acts 15? To this query we must give three responses. First, Timothy was half-Jewish, not fully Gentile, so Paul was simply normalizing his status one way or the other. Second, the circumcision debate was about Gentiles' salvation and spiritual status, while this passage is about mission and cultural identification. Finally, Luke is able to show that while Paul took a strong stand on primary theological issues, he could be flexible on a practical level as needed.

Struggling With Guidance (16:6-10)

Soon, however, the mission team pressed beyond familiar territory into new regions. If you have ever wondered how God is leading you, you are not alone. Paul had never ministered in new areas without Barnabas before. Normally, he had contacts arranged, such as Barnabas's contacts in Cyprus and probably those suggested by Sergius Paullus in Phrygia. Once Paul was the team leader and they entered new territory, depending on the Spirit to lead them, they seemed to wander almost aimlessly to the northeast. The Spirit gave them only negative guidance—where not to go—leaving them to press forward and wait for more positive guidance. Sometimes, as with the province of Asia, God's no is just for a season to prepare us for a more effective yes later.

Finally, when they reached the Roman colony of Alexandria Troas, they received positive guidance in the form of a dream. Neither God nor an angel spoke in the dream (as usually occurs in dreams described in the Bible); but they would step out on what they had, holding on to this memory of God's calling during the sufferings they would soon endure all the way through Macedonia. Happily, Troas was Asia Minor's best harbor for a voyage to Macedonia, and their voyage—here expedited by favorable seasonal winds—got underway.

Ancient hearers were likely to have caught the significance in this geographic transition, one we contemporary readers often miss. For Greeks, Troas represented a traditional boundary between what Greeks called Europe and what they called Asia. They told stories of Greek invasions of Asia there, such as the Trojan War and Alexander the Great's landing there. Here, however, the narrative reverses the Greek colonial tradition, and with it colonialist ideology. Ambassadors of peace were bringing the good news of Jesus Christ from Asia to Europe without weapons or cultural arrogance.

God Opens Hearts (16:11-15)

Traditionally, Paul had started in synagogues, where he found the most common ground; but Philippi did not have enough Jews for a synagogue. Thus they found a prayer meeting on the sabbath, attended by women interested in Judaism. In truth, Gentile women were more often interested in Judaism than men because of status issues and because men could not join the Jewish people without being circumcised.

The women welcomed teaching from Judean sages; and one of them, Lydia, welcomed them into her home. Hospitality was a crucial virtue in antiquity, one especially important for traveling Jews hoping to find lodging with fellow-Jews. Because most public inns doubled as brothels, consequently, enemies might have wished to seize on accepting cross-gender hospitality as scandalous. However, we should remember that Lydia had a household, Paul's team included several members (including the eyewitness source of Luke's "we" here, presumably Luke himself), and the house was probably fairly large.

Although Lydia may have sold fabrics dyed with cheaper imitation purple rather than the more expensive kind from Tyre, purple-dyed fabrics were luxury items; therefore she was probably fairly well-to-do, though not upper class. She may have even been a freed slave working for a business cooperative in the famous fabric industry of Thyatira (in the region of Lydia in Asia Minor, hence her name). Nevertheless, she offered Luke the opportunity to name another high-profile, respectable supporter of the faith.

Persecuted for Spiritual Liberation (16:16-22)

Soon, however, they encountered a slave girl with a Pythian spirit, who began identifying them as servants of the highest God. *Pythian* refers most often to the prophetess of Apollo at Delphi, the most famous oracle of the pagan world. Thus Gentiles would have respected this powerful prophetic spirit.

Nevertheless, Paul no more wanted a pagan spirit revealing his identity and mission than Jesus wanted the testimony of a spirit in a synagogue (Luke 4:33-35). So Paul cast out the spirit. The slaveholders who had been exploiting the girl were concerned only with their economic loss—just like the Gerasenes who chased Jesus away after the loss of their pigs—so they dragged Paul and Silas before the authorities in the city square.

Keep in mind that Philippi was a Roman colony, and its citizens were thereby automatically citizens of Rome. Under Roman law, a case like Paul's required his being brought before the local prosecutors. Of course Paul's accusers certainly knew that their charge of "property damage" might not stick, so they tried to stir up a mob by playing the race card. Ironically, Paul and Silas, who encountered persecution by other Jews, in this instance, faced persecution because they were Jews.

The Missionaries' Own Liberation (16:23-40)

After having the missionaries beaten with rods, the magistrates ordered the jailer to keep them securely. Complying fully, he placed these wounded men in the inner prison for the night. For good measure, they were also put in stocks. Leaving guards on duty, the jailer then retired for the night.

However, Paul and Silas refused to be deterred in their trust. They sang out loud in the middle of the night. (We do not learn the other prisoners' feelings about this. However, it is noteworthy that none of them

Paul: Roman Citizen

Some scholars have questioned whether Paul could have been a Roman citizen, complaining that this was a rare privilege for Jews. In fact, ancient sources show us that many Jews in Rome were Roman citizens; some of these migrated eastward. Like the majority of Jewish Roman citizens, Paul was probably descended from freed slaves of Roman citizens (his synagogue in 6:9).

Against complaints that Paul did not use his three Roman names in his letters, Jews barely ever did so (and many Gentiles did not either). In fact, the name *Paul* usually designated a Roman citizen; and Jewish parents had little reason to give this name to their son if he was not a citizen.

attempted escape, and Paul seemed in control of the situation in the prison). Earthquakes were not uncommon in that region, but this one precisely freed everyone without harming them. In contrast to Peter's two escapes earlier in Acts, Paul's story involved a miraculous non-escape!

The jailer, assuming that the prisoners must have escaped, was prepared to fall on his sword rather than face charges of negligence that he had not guarded them well enough. Paul intervened, and the jailer asked a standard question in Luke–Acts (asked elsewhere in similar words by crowds to John the Baptist and Peter, and by a wealthy ruler to Jesus): "What must I do to be saved?" Presumably, he had heard the report that, as the slave-girl had put it, these men were "preaching the way of salvation."

After the jailer and his family began trusting Jesus, he took them out of the jail and washed their wounds, in turn, submitting along with his family to the washing of baptism. For him to remove them from the jail and feed them violated all protocol, risking his livelihood. Luke' message is clear: Those who are genuinely converted make a real change in their lives. Paul and Silas also probably made an adjustment; it is not likely that the jailer had specifically kosher food on hand.

Whether due to the earthquake, the fact that cooler heads prevailed after the mob dispersed, or that a humiliating public beating and a night in jail was thought punishment enough, the authorities sent word to Paul that he was free to go. Yet Paul did not want to leave the new local church struggling with needless scandal, so he pointed out that his rights had been violated. He and Silas were Roman citizens, whom it was illegal to beat without trial.

Perhaps Paul waited until after the hearing to appeal to his citizenship to place the authorities in precisely this embarrassing predicament, perhaps the mob was too loud for him to get a hearing, or perhaps the jailer had explained to him that in Philippi he actually could get his rights this way. In any case, the embarrassed officials escorted them out, reducing at least some of their public dishonor. Yet the gospel of Jesus, thanks to Paul and his missionary team, had attracted much attention and some unlikely converts.

More Misery in Macedonia (17:1-14)

Paul and Silas walked westward on the main road (the Via Egnatia), their backs undoubtedly still sore from their bloody beating. Elsewhere in Macedonia, also, the apostles were run out of town in Thessalonica and Berea. In Thessalonica, Paul was even charged with preaching Jesus' kingship in competition against Caesar—the capital offense of treason.

Luke hoped that his audience would catch the connection between the false charges against Paul and the false charge against Jesus (Luke 23:2), who was supposedly "opposing the payment of taxes to Caesar." Paul was no more guilty than Jesus was; for Jesus' present kingdom belongs to a different dimension that impinges on this world without yet ending all of its political structures. Yet from Paul's own correspondence with the Thessalonians, it is clear that he did in fact expect God's kingdom to eventually overthrow worldly kingdoms in rebellion against God.

Reasoning With Other Intellectuals (17:15-34)

The situation began to change for Paul in the famous free city of Athens. Here, Paul's heart was stirred when he saw the idols worshiped by these otherwise intelligent people. We know from ancient descriptions that idols stood everywhere in Athens (not just on the temple-filled Acropolis, but in the markets below).

About the Scripture

Stoics and Epicureans

Stoic morality, in contrast to that of the Epicureans, had some overlap with Paul's beliefs, although there were also differences. Stoics emphasized self-control and a universal perspective, whereas Epicureans valued pleasure and the absence of pain. Stoics believed in Fate and the gods and that the chief mind had designed and inhabited the cosmos. Epicureans rejected gods in the conventional sense. Stoics believed that the cosmos was periodically dissolved by fire and reconstituted. Paul's speech at the Areopagus would have appealed to Stoic hearers at points, but it undoubtedly drew scorn from the Epicureans.

Talking in the marketplace with his hearers, including philosophers, Paul sought to help them understand his message; but these brilliant thinkers could not understand him. Some apparently thought he was preaching two deities, Jesus and Resurrection (in Greek, *anastasis*, the word translated as "resurrection," was a woman's name). Charging him with preaching "foreign deities"—the charge that led to Socrates's death in Athens centuries earlier—they brought him to Athens' high court, the Areopagus, probably to determine whether he should be certified to teach his philosophy in Athens or not.

Many recognized Paul's speech to the Areopagus as a model of how to relate to others' beliefs without compromising one's own Christian convictions. Stoic thinkers could agree with most of what Paul said in the speech, although it was also biblical. Only toward the end of his speech did Paul go beyond dialogue and seek conversion, bringing up necessary and important points of difference.

Countering the accusation that he appealed to "foreign" gods, Paul started by appealing to the "unknown god." Centuries before, when sacrifices to named deities failed to stop a plague, Athenians built altars to unknown deities. Now Paul explained that this God had actually been near to them, though they had not recognized this God. Stoics would agree that this God did not depend on temples or sacrifices.

However, while philosophers sometimes demanded a sort of conversion, Paul's call to repentance toward the end of his speech would not have pleased much of his audience. Still more jarring, he spoke of Jesus' resurrection. When Greeks thought of raising (in a bodily sense), they would be more apt to imagine something like a modern monster movie with corpses walking around than a transformed body. Paul's critics mocked him, others welcomed further intellectual dialogue, but a few actually become believers—quite a remarkable accomplishment.

Struggles and Opportunities in Corinth (18:1-17)

Just some 50 miles (a couple days' walk) beyond the old university town of Athens lay the thriving commercial city of Corinth. Here Paul encountered Aquila and Priscilla, leather workers (or something like that; the precise meaning is debated) who had set up shop in Corinth after being expelled from Rome. Other evidence suggests that the emperor had expelled some or much of the Jewish community because of debates over a Jewish king, a "Christ." Ringleaders of the Christian faction, as Aquila and Priscilla may have been viewed, would have been significant targets.

People of the same trades often lived near one another and worked together. Although Paul devoted himself full-time to ministry once his companions came with more support, Paul was ready to do manual labor within the culture he was seeking to serve.

Across the Testaments

Sharing the Gospel on Common Ground

Paul's message remained biblical even in a speech directed toward philosophically literate pagans. Paul quoted Greek poets, yet alluded to Scripture and biblical language throughout. Scripture spoke of the Lord of heaven and earth and of God making all people from one original person (meaning that we are all related). Stephen had already quoted Isaiah about God not dwelling in temples made with hands. Moreover, Paul declared that God created humanity in the divine image to be God's children; God did not want humanity to try to return the favor! When we find common ground for dialogue, we should not neglect the biblical source for our own beliefs.

Paul's message divided another synagogue, and a wealthy God-fearer opened his home for a new house church near the synagogue. In contrast to the Macedonian cities that ran him out, Paul was able to remain at length, working with the new church in Corinth.

Finally, his detractors brought him before Gallio, probably (based on what is known of Gallio's tenure) around A.D. 51–52. This governor was the brother of the famous philosopher Seneca, the young Nero's tutor. On this occasion, however, the charge backfired. Not only did Gallio refuse the case as irrelevant to Roman law—giving Paul a strategy he could use in his later trials—but he apparently tolerated an anti-Jewish outburst. The emperor's recent expulsion of Jews from Rome had set a bad example for others. Notice how extensive the risk and the potential were becoming for the spread of the gospel. So went the powerful work of the Holy Spirit in the world.

Acquiring Another Colleague (18:18-28)

Paul, Priscilla, and Aquila sailed for Ephesus. While Paul was out of town, another preacher named Apollos visited Ephesus; and Priscilla and Aquila provided him fuller teaching. (Note Priscilla's involvement in teaching and that she was named first. Husbands were normally named before wives unless the wife was of higher status. In this case she might have been of higher status in the church.)

Apollos went on to Corinth, making good use of his oratorical and biblical skills to strengthen the Christian community there. Here, as elsewhere in Acts, we see mission partnerships that spread the gospel more widely by lovingly working together.

Live the Story

Some of us are highly social—we thrive on being with other people. Others of us actually prefer spending time alone. Ultimately, however, at least as Christian witnesses in our world, we all flourish better if we find at least a few partners in our faith, people who support us and assist us in carrying out our mission for Christ.

Think of the various colleagues with whom Paul worked in this section of Acts. Think about what they did together. The point should be clear: Church is not just about holding services. It is about community, about functioning as members of Christ's body in conjunction with other members.

Think of ways we can join with one another today to serve and build healthy, life-giving relationships. Think also of some of the hardships that Paul and his companions endured.

What do their sacrificial lifestyles say to us? What are areas where we can learn to sacrifice gladly for the greater cause of God's work of serving people and bringing them the good news?

6.

Paul in Ephesus:
The Gospel and the Greeks

Acts 19–20

Claim Your Story

Have you ever felt discouraged or enraged by injustice, exploitation, and false ideologies in this world? Have you ever despaired of being able to make a difference?

In his book *Good News About Injustice: A Witness of Courage in a Hurting World*, Gary Haugen of the International Justice Mission recounts the struggle of Kate Bushnell in the 1880's. In northern Wisconsin and Michigan, many women were being forced into prostitution. The odds against ending this travesty were enormous. Despite grave danger, Bushnell had to infiltrate the brothels to gather evidence, interviewing hundreds of these enslaved women. The male authorities denied her claims and accused her of deceit and immorality. In time, however, other studies followed hers, exposing and ending this exploitation.

From Elijah to Jeremiah to Francis Asbury, many of God's servants have felt like giving up. Yet faithful perseverance can always make a difference. We may have to start small, doing what we can do; but no matter what we are up against, the claims of the gospel call for us to remain faithful to truth and justice. Just as the good news of Christ can change people, it can also change culture.

Enter the Bible Story

Although Acts 18 records Paul first coming to Ephesus, the bulk of Chapters 19 and 20 chronicle his long stay there (over two years), a stay that led to cultural shifts and to a backlash.

Finding Culturally Relevant Teaching Venues (19:1-20)

Shortly after his arrival, Paul met a group of 12 disciples who had not experienced the Spirit or received baptism with respect to Jesus' name. Scholars debate the passage's particulars, but it is at least clear that Paul counted as essential the experience of the Spirit and the centrality of the Lord Jesus.

As in other locations, Paul began his ministry in a synagogue, where he found the most common ground for discussing Jesus. The synagogue was divided over the issue of Jesus' identity. Eventually, Paul and those who agreed with him were forced to withdraw. However, Paul was ready for a strategy that could help him reach Gentiles as well as Jews. In Acts 16, the Spirit would not let him enter the Roman province of Asia. Because of his time in Greece, Paul was ready for the most effective phase of his public ministry: taking the gospel message to Ephesus, the chief city of Roman Asia.

Paul began teaching in the lecture hall of Tyrannus. He understood Greek culture (which dominated Ephesus) well enough to know the strategic ways to get a hearing, something like being media-savvy today. Philosophic sages holding schools could be well-respected; and Paul, who had already talked with philosophers in Athens, spoke as a sage, offering a new way of thought. Though modern history has sometimes driven a wedge between intellect and dependence on God's power, Paul demonstrated a sage through whom God brought healing and spiritual deliverance.

Success, however, breeds imitators, who do not always share the same genuine power as the authentic cases they imitate. Some traveling exorcists, noting Paul's success in using Jesus' name, tried to employ it themselves. Many people believed that using a more powerful spirit's name enabled one to control or expel less powerful spirits, so they were essentially

About the Scripture

Ephesian Artemis

The specifically Ephesian version of the goddess Artemis was worshiped from Syria to Spain at well over 30 sites known to us. Metalworkers sometimes made souvenir shrines, miniature replicas of temples. Silver was among the most expensive substances used for such souvenirs.

Artemis's temple, meanwhile, was famous throughout the Mediterranean world. Though smaller than Jerusalem's Temple for the one God, Artemis's temple was one of the largest in antiquity, about four times the size of Athens' Parthenon. It was regularly counted among the seven wonders of the ancient world, and its treasury (which doubled as a bank) attracted international depositors. A scandal in A.D. 44, about a decade before this incident, involved misappropriation of funds at the treasury, making the mixture of religion and economics a volatile combination in Ephesus in precisely this period.

exploiting Jesus' name as a magical formula. Some who did so were in for a serious surprise.

Word quickly spread that the name of Jesus was no mere formula, subject to its users' whim. That is, it was not enough just to know that Paul did miracles; it was important to know that these differed in kind from the other familiar acts of power to which people had been comparing them. As a result, people (including some who had already professed Christ) who had depended on magical writings and amulets publicly repudiated their magical texts by burning them. This passage reiterates that the message spread among Jews and Greeks in all of Asia (19:10, 17, 20).

Threatening Local Religious Exploitation (19:21-41)

Like Jesus resolving to go to Jerusalem in Luke's Gospel (Luke 9:51), Paul determined by the Spirit that he had to go on to Jerusalem and Rome (Acts 19:21). After he had already felt that his work in Ephesus was about finished, circumstances expedited his removal. In a speech full of exaggeration, Demetrius, maker of silver shrines, whipped his hearers into a frenzy. His complaint was two-fold. First, Paul was a threat to their religious livelihood. There was truth in this accusation; transforming individuals' lives and faith did impact society. Less than a century later, a governor in Asia Minor complained that the temples of the gods were being forsaken because of Christians. Likewise, Christian conversions sometimes have secured the enmity of drug dealers, slaveholders, and others who thrive on exploiting others. This economic basis for opposing Paul escalated the sort of threat that occurred in Philippi when slaveholders could no longer profit by exploiting a slave whom Paul delivered from a spirit.

Second, Paul was a threat to the honor of the patron goddess of Ephesus because he claimed that deities made with hands were not genuine. There is truth here as well. Paul's speech before the Areopagus shows that he did preach such things. Here, however, this is viewed not as a new idea or a minority (Jewish) religion but as a threat to local religious pride.

The public market was beside the theater, and a crowd was quickly brought into the theater, perhaps supposing that they were being called into an emergency meeting of the town assembly. In fact, as will soon be pointed out, this riot was an illegal gathering, for which Rome had little tolerance.

The mob had seized two of Paul's companions, and Paul wanted to take the opportunity to address the crowd. Had Paul addressed the crowd, he would have undoubtedly been shouted down. A representative of the synagogue community tried to address the crowd, perhaps to dissociate their personal monotheism from Paul's public preaching of it. He was shouted down; and the synagogue community, already upset because Paul had split the synagogue, may have felt that they were being blamed for Paul's riot. It is not too surprising, then, that some Jews from Ephesus would later misrepresent Paul as being against his people and instigating riots.

Finally, the town clerk (one of the chief officials of Ephesus) quieted the crowd, publicly reproved Demetrius, and defended Paul's companions as not having blasphemed the goddess. After all, he insisted, their preaching against "deities made with hands" could not apply to Artemis, whose image was not handmade, but fell from heaven fully

About the Christian Faith

Faith in Action: Contemporary Heroes

Throughout history, some Christians, motivated by their faith, have recognized needs for justice and mercy in society and determined to meet those needs. William Wilberforce devoted his life to the abolition of slavery until, while he lay on his deathbed, slavery was finally abolished in the British Empire. The United States saw faith-inspired abolitionists such as Harriet Tubman, Sojourner Truth, and Arthur and Lewis Tappan. After abolition, there were reformers such as Ida B. Wells and Amanda Berry Smith.

Likewise, Kate Bushnell fought 19th-century sex trafficking in the United States, a fore-runner of those battling such exploitation and enslavement internationally today. Scholar and reformer Pandita Ramabai advocated in India for widows and, after becoming a Christian, the position of women in general. William and Catherine Booth, founders of the Salvation Army, carried forward the Wesleyan vision of social transformation alongside evangelism.

Today groups such as International Justice Mission, Bread for the World, and World Vision continue to challenge injustices and inequities, bringing to bear their faith in a world of desperate need.

formed. Luke's audience, however, knew better. Yet even Luke could not have known that monotheism would ultimately supplant the Artemis cult in Ephesus someday.

Suspense Builds en Route to Jerusalem (20:1-16)

From Paul's New Testament letters we learn that Paul's following journey to Jerusalem involved a collection for the poor there, showing the solidarity of the Diaspora churches with the needs of their fellow believers in Judea. For some reason, however, Luke alludes to this collection only once, with little detail. Some scholars think that Luke ignored it because it did not accomplish what Paul had hoped; others think that he ignored it because it was simply not important by his day. Clearly Luke remained interested in the church's cross-cultural unity and in caring for the poor, both themes in his work. In any case, Luke reported other important incidents en route. He reported these in greater detail, apparently, because he was there (hence "we").

In Troas, Paul spoke all night long, because he had to leave in the morning, and this provided his only chance to teach the disciples there. His sermon was so long that a young man, Eutychus, fell asleep and fell to his death, providing Paul an occasion for a miracle to accompany his message.

Warning the Church (20:17-35)

Paul also addressed the elders from Ephesus in the nearby city of Miletus. His speech there sounds more like his letters than any of his other speeches in Acts, perhaps partly because Luke was there in person to take more detailed notes, and partly because this was Paul's only speech in Acts where he was addressing a church (as in his letters).

As at times in his letters, Paul offered his own ministry as an example for those serving the church. Paul had suffered for them and sacrificed for them. He faced opposition, worked hard to provide financial support to the mission and to reach out to each person, and explained about Jesus to believers and nonbelievers without compromising the truth to satisfy what anyone might want to hear. He spoke publicly and in private to Jews and Greeks. That same commitment drove him to risk his life in Jerusalem, because all that mattered to him was fulfilling what God had called him to do.

Paul's concern about what might await him in Jerusalem was not paranoia. The Holy Spirit, presumably through prophecies in various cities (as in Acts 21), kept warning him of what awaited him. Yet Paul's purpose was not to live a comfortable life; it was to make his life count eternally for God's purposes. Simply because a course of action seems costly does not mean that it is not God's will.

However, Paul's departure also meant that other servants of the church needed to take full responsibility for it. Paul's example summoned them to sacrificial vigilance on behalf of God's people. He warned of scandals. Some church leaders would prove insincere, preying on the flock. (The image of wolves attacking sheep was a common one in Paul's day, literally and

---

Biblical Metaphors: Shepherd and Flock

When Paul spoke of the church as God's flock, he drew on rich imagery from Israel's history. The community of Israel in the wilderness was called the *qahal*, and one of the Greek terms Jewish people used to translate this word was *ekklesia*, the New Testament term for "church." (It was also the term used for civic assemblies. The other term used to translate *qahal* was *synagoge*, already in use for synagogues.)

Scripture often called Israel God's "flock" and God its chief shepherd. Moreover, others also were called to "shepherd" Israel under God, including Moses and David. Sometimes God reproved Israel's leaders for their failure to care for the flock rightly, warning that God, the Chief Shepherd, would defend the flock. Those familiar with the struggles of Israel's ancient leaders will also recognize that Paul faced some of the same struggles, as we often do today.

---

figuratively.) We all know that some leaders, less than whole themselves, have abused their positions to exploit others emotionally, sexually, or financially. It would be the responsibility of sincere leaders to watch out for such persons and to guard the flock no matter what the cost to themselves. God's servants must love and serve the church, never taking their responsibility lightly. Paul entrusted his church leaders to God's word.

Finally, Paul returned again to his own example. In his day, as in ours, many complained of charlatan teachers out to exploit others financially. An early Christian document, the Didache, even specifies requests for money as a means of discerning false prophets! (While exaggerated—ministers do need support—the warning does remind us where our priorities should lie.) Paul, however, had lived sacrificially, working manually to help support his ministry team.

Affection and Spiritual Warnings (20:36–21:14)

Paul's departure shows (as do various other scenes in the following chapters) how much people who knew Paul loved him. Sometimes we miss the tone in Paul's writings, unfamiliar with the forms of debate, persuasion, and affection in his culture. Yet we cannot miss the affection that those who knew and understood him had for him, because they knew that he cared about them.

Such scenes continue in Chapter 21 as Paul continued on his way to Jerusalem. Through the Spirit, some warned Paul not to enter Jerusalem. Here is the ambiguity of spiritual gifts and spiritual guidance: They were right that trouble awaited him, but he was also right to go. What they discerned spiritually was partial rather than complete. Paul said, "We know in part and we prophesy in part" (1 Corinthians 13:9). Again, however, we see the people's love for Paul.

The next scene displays this pattern still more eloquently. The group stayed with Philip the evangelist, who had now settled in Caesarea. (Philip could well be a major source for Luke's earlier chapters in Acts, especially since Luke would soon spend a long time in Caesarea while Paul was in Roman custody there.) His four young daughters illustrated the point of Peter's Pentecost prophecy: Daughters as well as sons, and young as well as old, would prophesy.

They were soon joined by Agabus, a veteran prophet from Jerusalem, who warned what Paul would face there. Again, everyone (including Luke and apparently Philip and his daughters) tried to deter Paul from his mission. When Paul insisted, they gave in, accepting God's will as Jesus did in Gethsemane. Giving people a chance to receive the good news of Jesus is worth whatever price it will cost us.

Live the Story

Will our different lives and message ever challenge a culture that lives by different values? Paul was not trying to stir a riot or even address politics in Ephesus, but Ephesian politics was so intertwined with pagan values that conflict could not be avoided. Paul's message of a God not made with hands challenged exploitive religious practices on which a significant part of Ephesus' economy was based.

Our culture today is no less prone to exploitive religious practice than Ephesus was. Consider how much Christianity in the United States is driven by consumerism and marketing, just like the rest of the culture.

While marketing can be a useful tool, some things sell better than truth. You can probably think of other issues where religion, politics, economic structures, or other matters mislead and exploit people. Entrenched interests do not easily give way to others' moral or religious convictions. Where have you seen that to be true?

Serving even God's people sometimes comes with a price. Some people do not necessarily want to be served or ministered to or loved in the name of Jesus; and like children, they often rebel against their best interests.

Take a moment to consider your role in your church. How might Paul's example help you to serve God and others more fully, especially when your service is met with opposition or antagonism?

7.

Paul on the Defense

Acts 21–24

Claim Your Story

Have you ever wondered what the rules of the game are? Have you ever met people who are so sure that they know the rules that they don't mind stepping on others to achieve their goals? Even in the realm of faith, some people seem surer of themselves than others. Of course, this assurance is a good thing when it grows from a humble relationship with God. However, when an overdose of self-assurance manifests itself in the form of religious bigotry or a defense of traditions beyond the bounds of biblical faith, it can be harmful.

In the readings for this session, we will see two different pictures of religion. In one case, religion is exploited in the service of nationalistic objectives. In the other, a heart driven by the gospel of Christ is committed to the good news being for all peoples.

In the first instance, the church in Jerusalem was so focused on its own culture that many were ready to believe the worst about Paul. They wanted Paul to identify with their own mission in Jerusalem, rather than look outward to his mission to the Gentiles. Paul, on the other hand, used yet another occasion of personal suffering—at the hands of his fellow Jews, no less—to find strength to continue his mission to bring the gospel of Jesus to all.

While you are reading, call to mind occasions when your faith has met with opposition. Think about what has fortified you in those moments.

Enter the Bible Story

Although Paul was committed to the Gentiles, he had not stopped loving his own people. He was ready to identify with them as well. The leaders of the Jerusalem church welcomed Paul and his companions —including the Gentiles—but apparently got right down to business. The leaders were not reneging on their earlier agreement regarding the Gentiles, but they wanted to refute rumors that Paul was against Jewish people retaining their own traditions. Abuses by corrupt Roman governors had only fueled Judean nationalism further, and these cultural values shaped Judeans who were members of the church as well. Most of them had only negative experiences of Gentiles; and in that conservative social environment, many were ready to believe the hostile rumors about Paul.

Paul agreed to show his solidarity with his people, offering sacrifices in the Temple. Even our best-intentioned plans can, however, be misinterpreted at times. Luke's narrative shows how all of this nevertheless fit into God's larger plan of getting Paul to Rome.

Beaten for a False Accusation (21:15-40)

Ironically, in the midst of identifying with his people, Paul was accused of doing the opposite. Sometimes we can learn from others' criticisms of us, but false accusations against us and our motives are also a reality that we must learn to handle graciously. Some Jews from the area of Ephesus, having recognized an Ephesian Gentile with Paul in Jerusalem, presumed that Paul had brought this man into the Temple. Signs posted at the Temple's entrances warned that any Gentile who passed the outer court would be responsible for his or her own ensuing death. By charging Paul with desecrating the Temple, they fomented a riot not unlike the earlier one in Ephesus. Building suspense, their charges were much like the charges that got Stephen martyred.

Just above the outer court of the Temple stood the Fortress Antonia, where the city's Roman garrison was stationed to control riots and the like. Undoubtedly they were especially alert during this season (near the festival of Pentecost) and because of a number of recent assassinations in the Temple. Seeing the commotion, the soldiers rushed down the stairway into the outer court and seized Paul. This mob, like the one in Acts 19, was confused, with different views of why they were attacking Paul anyway.

The tribune, commander of the cohort in the Antonia—and himself Greek by birth—was surprised to hear Paul's "good" Greek accent. He had wrongly identified Paul with the above-mentioned Egyptian Jew. Greeks and Romans in this period did not normally think highly of Egyptians. Paul explained that he was, rather, a Tarsian Jew whom the crowd had misunderstood and offered to explain himself to the crowd.

Following Jesus Includes Welcoming Gentiles (22:1-29)

In contrast to the riot in Ephesus, Paul would not be deterred from addressing the people this time. When the Judeans heard him speaking Aramaic—something his Ephesian detractors probably could not even understand—they listened. They heard him out as he recounted his conversion story, emphasizing his solidarity with his people.

Yet his speech concluded with a call to the Gentiles—perhaps Jerusalem's last public chance to turn from their nationalistic fervor before the revolt that would lead, as Jesus warned in Luke's Gospel, to the city's tragic devastation. Jesus' movement had gained many adherents in Jerusalem over the years; and had Paul stopped his Pentecost speech—like Peter a generation before—by simply calling people to turn to Jesus, he might have won a sympathetic crowd. However, for Paul, the true gospel of Jesus included transformation; and this required a degree of ethnic and cultural reconciliation that their nationalism could not accommodate.

The Jerusalem church was no longer persecuted as much. It had been successful in identifying with their culture and represented the most obvious megachurch of its day, in contrast to the Bible study groups Paul was laboring to start around the Empire. Yet in identifying with its culture—to which Paul had no objection—this church had also failed to challenge its culture's exclusivism and nationalism. These attitudes were understandable; but Paul, while willing to identify, was not willing to be silent about truth.

Who could have foreseen that within less than a decade, Jerusalem's church would be scattered and Paul's churches would represent the model for the future? Even if what God gives us to do seems smaller than what God gives someone else to do, we should work for God faithfully, trusting the Lord for the outcome.

Once Paul revealed that Jesus had sent him to the Gentiles, the riot started again. Deciding that Paul was the source of the riot after all, the tribune ordered him interrogated by torture. However, Paul protested his citizenship before he could be flogged. Suddenly the tribune was in an uncomfortable situation. Lysias had chained a Roman citizen without a trial. How did Paul get his citizenship? Unfortunately for Lysias, Paul was a citizen by birth, conferring on him an unexpectedly high status in the eastern Mediterranean, where fewer people held the franchise.

Dividing the Sanhedrin (22:30–23:10)

Governors could sometimes afford to ignore the rules, but a politically ambitious tribune could not. At the same time, he could not refer Paul to the governor without understanding the charges against him. Lysias thus decided to bring in the highest governing body in Jerusalem for consultation. There, undoubtedly to Lysias's astonishment, he witnessed the high priest ordering Paul to be struck. Paul answered from Scripture. His identification with his people through Scripture appeared to stir no interest, so Paul tried a different tack. As he had previously appealed more to Stoic hearers than Epicureans in Athens, here he used "divide and conquer" to secure at least some allies in the Sanhedrin.

Pharisees were probably a minority in the Sanhedrin, but Paul identified with them because of their common affirmation of the resurrection of the dead, marginalized by the powerful Sadducees. (Paul undoubtedly spoke Greek so that Lysias could understand.) Jesus' resurrection was at the heart of the preaching in Acts, and Paul's message depended on this claim. By shifting the argument to a claim that he knew could not stand under Roman law, Paul skillfully guarded his future case. Meanwhile, the Pharisees, presumably having heard reports of Paul's testimony of Jesus' appearance (from his speech in the Temple), were willing to entertain

The Sanhedrin in Paul's Day

Two generations earlier, Herod the Great had eliminated local political opposition by simply executing much of the old Sanhedrin and filling the new one with his own political supporters. These families known to be supportive of Herod and Rome's interests remained in power in this period. Josephus, a Jewish historian active in this period, reported plots and intrigues (including a plot from Sanhedrin leaders against himself). At another point in this period, members of the Sanhedrin began throwing rocks at one another. He reported that some members of high priestly families were involved in assassinations of others. Other historians reported scenes of conflict in other local senates, including the Roman Senate. Luke's description is therefore believable—a description of how power can corrupt those who hold it.

that Paul had some sort of experience with a deceased person's spirit or angel.

When Lysias witnessed the two factions ready to tear Paul apart, he again intervened. He had discovered several things: First, Paul was quite controversial; he was a political hot potato better deferred to the governor. Second, the charges against Paul were religious ones, not anything relevant to Roman law.

Eluding Assassins (23:11-32)

The Lord assured Paul that he was with him and would fulfill his witness at Rome as well. The need for this encouragement was soon evident. A number of young Judean nationalists were at this time involved in low-level resistance against Rome that would turn into a full-scale revolt a few years later. Some such nationalists banded together to kill Paul, ironically with no less religious zeal (here displayed in a vow and a fast) than he had once displayed. They arranged with contacts in the Sanhedrin to ask that Paul be brought to the Sanhedrin. Between the Fortress Antonia, where he was being kept, and the usual meeting hall of the Sanhedrin, was probably less than 1,500 feet. Some of the way was fairly narrow, and a surprise attack could kill Paul before it could be stopped. Providentially, Paul had a nephew in Jerusalem, probably in the same age bracket, who warned Paul about the plot.

Paul made sure that his nephew informed Lysias—keeping everything secret, probably so that Lysias would not need to take sides publicly and especially to keep Paul's nephew safe. Then Lysias sent what was probably the majority of the garrison under cover of night to ensure that Paul was brought safely to the governor. The cavalry could engage in quick action; but the infantry provided the numbers in case of any surprise attack along narrow paths in the Judean hills, which had become notoriously dangerous. Lysias staked everything on Paul's safe arrival, determined not to lose the escort in the process.

Roman armies were accustomed to periodic forced marches. After the contingent reached the safer (and more Gentile) Judean plain, the foot soldiers returned back to guard the Antonia while the cavalry rode on in daylight to bring Paul to Caesarea. Because Lysias's letter would become part of Paul's official court record, he wisely left out reference to any involvement by Jerusalem's leaders. This information could be conveyed to the governor more discreetly.

Accused Before the Governor (23:33–24:21)

Felix, the governor, held his position because his brother Pallas was an influential freedman serving the emperor in Rome. In his lifetime, Felix married three princesses. His current wife was Drusilla, the Jewish sister of Agrippa II and Bernice, so he had some knowledge of Jewish affairs. Recognizing immediately that Paul's case could be politically difficult, he inquired concerning Paul's province, hoping to send him to his home governor for trial. Cilicia was at this time united with Syria, however, which meant that the chief governor, the governor of Syria, was Felix's immediate boss; and he might not appreciate the intrusion. So Felix had to handle the case.

Soon Paul's high-status accusers arrived with a forensic orator who could denounce Paul eloquently. Tertullus's denunciation fit typical accusatory rhetoric of the day and was longer on assertions than proof. That Paul was accused of stirring riots everywhere was a serious charge, one that

Luke himself was eager to refute. (Luke reports numerous riots surrounding Paul but shows that they were always started by others. Given what we know about Paul, it is unlikely that he went around starting riots.)

Paul's response offered such a strong case that Felix should have released him except for the political inexpediency of further alienating leaders in Jerusalem. (Felix often differed with them but eventually would be recalled based on their demands.) Paul began by showing that logically he could not have come to Jerusalem to cause trouble. Too many witnesses could attest to his recent movements that would not have fit that paradigm. Paul thus established that he was an honorable person who would not desecrate the Temple; in fact, he brought offerings to the Temple.

As it was customary to return charges against one's opponents, Paul pointed out that his original accusers had abandoned the case after being the ones to initiate it. Under Roman law, therefore, the case ought to have been dropped or the accusers themselves arraigned.

Eventually Paul invited his accusers to report the outcome of his preliminary hearing before the Sanhedrin, where the only real charge was that he supported the Resurrection. His enemies came with different charges than were offered at that hearing, but changing charges in the midst of a trial was illegal. He showed that it was obvious that his opponents acted in bad faith and that the real charge was a theological one, hence one in which Rome had no interest.

Politics Versus Justice (24:22-27)

Had Felix acted with integrity at this point, Paul would have been freed; but Felix had politics to be concerned with. As in the case of Jesus before Pilate, provincial political considerations trumped justice, as we know historically they often did and as they do in much of the world today. This Roman citizen had a constituency (this "Nazarene" sect) that could complain if Felix handed an obviously innocent man over. Conversely, Jerusalem's elite constituted a powerful constituency with whom he was already on poor terms. So Felix procrastinated, leaving Paul in nice conditions, but still in custody.

About the Scripture

Caesarea Maritima: Paul's Prison by the Sea

According to Acts 23:12–26:22, Paul spent two years in a prison in the coastal city of Caesarea, a city he had already visited at the close of his second journey, on his way to Jerusalem and Antioch (Acts 18:22). Built by Herod the Great, Caesarea-by-the-Sea was a vital Mediterranean seaport boasting a magnificent artificial harbor, a marvel of human engineering.

Once Judea became a Roman province in A.D. 6, the governors appointed by the Roman emperor all ruled from Caesarea, living in what was originally Herod's royal palace. It was from Caesarea that Pontius Pilate would have come to Jerusalem to preside over the trial of Jesus. In fact, a piece of archaeological evidence supporting Pilate's existence and authority was discovered on a block of limestone excavated at Caesarea in 1961: The brief inscription on the stone reads, "Tiberium Pontius Pilate, Prefect of Judea."

Paul remained in custody for about two years (though this is probably ancient reckoning for parts of two years). What was Luke doing during these two years? At least one line of his work was probably collecting accounts that would later comprise his Gospel. Finally, Felix was recalled to Rome because of complaints about maladministration. Even governors could go too far.

Driven by nationalism in the guise of religious tradition, Paul's opponents were blinded to the reality of his experience with God. Paul, however, had met God in Jesus Christ and knew that God welcomed Jew and Gentile alike in his family through Jesus Christ.

Less focused on his own defense than on the opportunity to preach Christ, Paul kept shifting the focus back to the heart of the real issue: He was being persecuted for preaching Jesus' resurrection, the issue for which he was genuinely prepared to die. He remained faithful to this message in the face of hostility from religious and political leaders because he was committed to the truth he knew through having met Jesus Christ. He did not disdain others or lash out at them; he reasoned with them, humbly wishing to offer them the gift he had received.

Live the Story

To read these chapters in Acts as merely a conflict between Jewish and Christian tradition is to miss the point. Paul himself was Jewish, and the temptation to abuse religion to vindicate one's own people as over against others is not limited to any one people or religious group. Standing for a God who loves everyone can sometimes bring us into conflict with people, even today—particularly those who bend faith, sometimes even our Christian faith, to serve other agendas.

What groups of people are you (or your church) most comfortable serving or reaching? What groups of people are you (or your church) uncomfortable serving or reaching? When have you ever felt uncomfortable with Christians who use a different style of ministry or angle of approach to reach certain groups of people with the gospel? When have you ever judged people's motives before hearing them out?

Consider this: The next time an opportunity to discuss your Christian faith comes along, think of your faith not as a possession to protect, but as a gift to be given. See how that affects the conversation.

8.

The Gospel Reaches Rome

Acts 25–28

Claim Your Story

I was converted to Christian faith from unchurched atheism. I was convinced that Christians were quite simply unintelligent, but then again I barely knew what they believed. The first time some bold Christians tried to share the gospel, I argued with them for forty-five minutes and finally walked off. These earnest Christians did not learn until a year later that I became a Christian not long after I had left them that very afternoon. Nothing I have accomplished in the past few decades as a Christian would have ever happened if those Christians had not been bold enough to risk ridicule and rejection to share Christ with people who did not know him. Even if I were the only one who responded to their message that day, the fruit of their ministry has multiplied through mine in the years that followed.

John Wesley and the early Methodists were similarly passionate about reaching everyone with the gospel, so much so that despite persecution and hardship, they traveled throughout the countryside to bring the message to everyone possible. So where is our passion as Christians today?

Most of us have little if any experience being persecuted for being Christian. Many of us would find unbearable the prospect of speaking about our faith to an antagonistic or unreceptive hearer. As you read the closing chapters of Acts, reflect on the story of these first believers; and compare their experiences with what you have experienced in your life of faith. Ask yourself, Where is my passion? Who do I know who might need to see the gospel lived out in my life or hear about the love of Jesus in my own words?

Enter the Bible Story

An Apostle's Appeal and a Governor's Consultation (25:1-22)

More efficient and dutiful than Felix, Porcius Festus (his replacement) traveled to Jerusalem shortly after his arrival to meet the local elite. There they requested that Paul be brought to Jerusalem for trial, and Festus resisted. Especially given his predecessor's recall following local complaints, Festus had good reason to grant them a political favor on a minor case; but Festus upheld Roman protocol, requiring an official hearing first.

To Festus's dismay, the charges offered at the official hearing proved unsubstantiated; but he wanted to grant the officials the favor of a hearing in Jerusalem. In view of the earlier assassination plot against Paul, a "hearing" in Jerusalem would seem to be a virtual death sentence. Thus Paul evaded such a hearing by using his Roman citizenship to appeal to Caesar.

Although governors often referred Roman citizens to Rome after an initial hearing, appeals more often followed a negative verdict. Festus thus confered with his consilium (his small council of advisors), who concurred that an appeal at an earlier stage, even if unusual, was legal. Festus clearly had reasons to desire to comply. The elite in Jerusalem wanted Paul executed, yet Paul seemed to be innocent.

By referring the matter to Rome, Festus passed on a political hot potato. Yet Festus could not easily send on a prisoner without noting a legal opinion, even though he had not convicted him; and his own consilium would not be qualified to help him formulate an opinion informed about the nature of the Jewish legal charges. Therefore, he made use of a formal visit by Agrippa II (son of Herod Agrippa I, who died in Acts 12) and his sister Bernice. He mentioned the case politely, implicitly soliciting his opinion. Agrippa, who must have had considerable knowledge about the local Christian movement, welcomed the opportunity to hear Paul and to contribute to Festus's formal letter of opinion.

Paul's Defense of the Good News (25:23–26:32)

In the midst of tribunes and civic leaders, Agrippa and Bernice entered the hall with great pomp that contrasted with God's representa-

Agrippa and Bernice

Agrippa and Bernice, children of Herod Agrippa I, were Hellenized and Romanized, inviting Festus to trust them as rational sources for explaining Judean customs and ideas. Although respected by his own people, he also remained loyal to Rome, even during the Judean revolt. Though young, Agrippa II was politically shrewd. Like other politicians, he visited and congratulated new officials. Josephus portrays Agrippa having a good working relationship with Festus but some tension with the aristocratic priests in Jerusalem.

Their father gave Bernice to a politically prominent man in marriage when she was 13; and after his decease he married her to her elderly uncle when she was 16, soon leaving her widowed again. She was close to her brother Agrippa and stayed with him for several years (leading to false rumors of incest). Her marriage to a Gentile king afterward quickly broke up, and she became famous for her long affair with the emperor's son Titus.

tive in chains. Here Paul pleaded his case—or rather, the case of his message. Paul was no longer at risk of being sent to Jerusalem. Now he had to establish the religious grounds on which the case depended.

After Paul had narrated the events leading up to his detention, he began offering evidence from Scripture. At this point it was clear that Paul was not merely defending himself but trying to persuade his hearers as to the truth of his claims. Festus, who already confessed to the royal visitors his perplexity regarding Paul's views, now interjected that Paul's great learning (probably in the Scriptures) had driven him insane. So Paul appealed to Agrippa to confirm that what he had been saying from Scripture was accurate. Agrippa likewise rebuffed him, critiquing Paul's desire to convert him. Paul wittily retorted that he would in fact like Agrippa to have what he had—minus, of course, the chains.

Festus and his royal guests conferred privately, but Luke knew their discussion based on the outcome: a supporting letter for Rome declaring the formal opinion that Paul was innocent, despite highly placed charges against him.

About the Scripture

Risky Shipping in Paul's Day

Egypt was the bread basket of the Roman Empire, and merchant ships carrying its grain plied the Mediterranean. In fact, Rome took as taxation so much of the grain that Egypt grew that many Egyptian children died of starvation and malnutrition, while Rome's resident citizens received a monthly allotment of grain free from the government. Merchants who could clear their grain in Italy in time for another trip naturally could make more money.

The previous emperor, Claudius, had encouraged ships to sail even in winter, which was dangerous, to keep Rome well-stocked with grain. The merchants often had to borrow money to buy their cargoes. The insurance arrangement, costing as much as 30 percent of the loan price, did not require them to repay in the case of shipwreck. Shipowners might be reluctant to jettison the cargo; but when the choice was between the cargo and their lives, people almost always chose to save their lives. The sailors, meanwhile, had little stake in such ships. They were poorly paid and often were the ship owners' slaves or slaves rented from others.

Risks at Sea (Chapter 27)

While the voyage to Rome may have delivered Paul from political opponents, Paul and his companions were in for unplanned adventure of another kind. With authority to requisition a place for himself and those traveling with him, Julius the centurion located a ship heading north. At another port they transferred to an Alexandrian ship heading west for Italy. Unfortunately, in the haste to get Paul out of Judea, the travelers were voyaging late in sailing season.

On average, sailing season was already risky between September 14 and November 11. From November 11 through March 10, only the most daring took to the seas. The travelers faced contrary winds from the northwest impeding their progress, continuing to seek shelter on southern coasts until they reached a small fishing village on the southern coast of Crete.

Those in charge of the ship had ulterior motives for wanting to sail quickly. The crew would not want to winter in a fishing village, with few available women or other interests there. The shipowner would want to get his cargo to Rome as quickly as possible, though a return voyage to Alexandria would probably have to await spring.

Soon after the ship had left harbor, however, an unexpected Euraquilo—a northeaster, considered the most dangerous wind—swept down on them. Because of local topography, they would not have seen the wind coming. Because they were unaccustomed to this route, they were not prepared to expect it. Those aboard took all possible measures to help themselves. During storms, people often lightened ships by throwing overboard whatever could be spared. While only some of the cargo was meant here (more was jettisoned later, and it could take days manually to unload such a large cargo ship), they did what they could.

Nevertheless, human measures are not always enough to help us. As many days passed, the passengers eventually abandoned hope (Acts 27:20). People in the ancient Mediterranean world considered death at sea one of the most horrible ways to die, partly because the person could have no burial. Many Gentiles believed that those who were not buried could not enter the afterworld, consigned instead to wander perpetually in the region of their death. Because Paul spoke the hard truth before, his words of encouragement should have carried more conviction when he communicated the angelic message that they would survive.

When the sailors realized that they were approaching land, they cast anchors to keep from running aground in the dark. Some sailors also wanted to enter a small boat to go outside and help maneuver the ship. A legitimate maneuver in such circumstances, it normally would not have been suspect had Paul not warned the soldiers otherwise.

Such a large ship might not have been able to reach land without grounding on underwater rocks before the shore, and only one small boat could ferry passengers ashore before the ship would sink. In that case, the soldiers, who were armed, would surely control the boat; hence the sailors hoped to escape with the boat. Without their expertise, however, the ship could not be protected long enough for the other passengers to escape; heeding Paul's concern, the soldiers cut away the best human hope available for rescuing any, apart from Paul being right. When our circumstances become too desperate to trust anything else, we may learn to trust and obey God more fully.

Paul, probably speaking to people huddled below deck, encouraged the passengers to eat. Whether they had been merely saving their food or were seasick, they would need strength to get ashore. Although some strict Judeans might not have approved of eating with the Gentiles, Paul ate with them in language reminiscent of the common meals of Jesus' followers.

By virtue of his relationship with God, Paul had gone from prisoner to respected leader; and this won him favor with the centurion as well. Possibly most of the prisoners were already condemned to be killed by beasts or gladiators for the Roman public's entertainment. The soldiers discussed killing them rather than risking liability for their escape, since they obviously could not swim in heavy chains. For Paul's sake, however, Julius spared all the prisoners. For Paul's sake, and the sake of his mission to testify before Caesar's court, God spared all the passengers.

God does not always spare us testing, but someone who genuinely serves God can live in confidence that God is watching over him or her. The sailors maneuvered the ship as close to land as the underwater reefs allowed. Miraculously, all 276 persons aboard, without exception, reached land safely.

Ministry in Malta (28:1-10)

Not all opportunities for ministry are planned. Often we are able to affect people who watch our lives and serve people we meet along the way. The people from the ship soon learned that the island was Malta (which apparently had a more suitable harbor perhaps seven miles from the place of their shipwreck).

Willing to help however he could in the poor weather, Paul was gathering sticks for a fire when a viper bit him. Many in antiquity believed that deities would exact justice by sinking ships to kill wicked persons; and if they escaped the sea, they would soon meet another fate. However, when God protected Paul even from this attack, the local people decided that Paul was divine.

Publius, a prominent estate owner with nearby land, hosted the centurion, Paul, and other persons of rank at his home. Paul offered a greater gift in return: Just as Jesus cured Peter's mother-in-law of fever, Paul cured Publius's father. When word spread, Paul's gift from God brought him to everyone's attention again. Luke wanted his audience to understand that even though Paul would be tried and eventually executed under Nero, he was a true servant blessed by God; and his compassionate mission to the Gentiles was the right way for the future.

Reasoning in Rome (28:11-31)

As they resumed the path to Rome again, Julius was again confronted with how this new movement pervaded the Empire and loved Paul, a leader in the Gentile mission. Once Paul settled in Rome, however, his first act was to call together the local Jewish leaders. This fit Paul's pattern: He always started with his own people.

Unlike synagogues in Alexandria and perhaps some other locations, Rome's synagogues were all autonomous. Most scholars believe that the Christian movement in Rome had started in synagogues there much earlier but that the emperor banished at least the Jewish Christian leaders—and possibly others—due to dissensions over the identity of the Messiah. As a respected leader and scholar in the early Christian movement, Paul received a hearing again for his message. However, the response, as throughout Acts, was divided.

Across the Testaments

Paul's Appeal to Moses and the Prophets

Luke quotes Scripture far less in Acts 16–28 than in preceding chapters, partly because more of the action occurred among Gentiles, but also partly because he had illustrated his approach to the Scriptures adequately in the earlier chapters. Nevertheless, even in this closing section, Paul often appealed to Moses and the prophets and to the hope of Israel.

In the closing scene of Acts, Luke elaborates one text at greater length: God's warning to Isaiah that Israel would be hard of heart. Isaiah was supposed to preach to Israel anyway, but the point of the analogy for Paul's day is self-evident: Even God's own people might resist, justifying Paul placing so much priority in sharing the good news with outsiders—the Gentiles.

The Book of Acts ends with Paul preaching openly as he remained under house arrest. Luke does not tell us what happened at the end of two years, perhaps partly because he wished to end on a pleasant note. Some scholars think that the hearing before Nero's court took an unexpectedly hostile turn; others believe that Paul was released, only to be rearrested a few years later and executed under Nero. Whichever case is true, Luke has already dropped plenty of hints that Paul was ready to lay down his life for the gospel.

Why does Acts end where it does? Undoubtedly it ends there partly because the good news had reached the very heart of the Empire. If it had reached Rome, the reader could be assured that it would also reach to the ends of the earth and was merely a foreshadow of where the gospel mission would take God's people. Who in the first century could have imagined that Christianity would for a time become the dominant faith of what is now Turkey and Egypt; soon thereafter of Ethiopia and Europe; and today the numerically dominant faith in Sub-Saharan Africa, Latin America, and the Philippines?

Of course, these rapid shifts warn us. Just as Paul declared that his own people could forfeit the favor of the gospel offered first to them, any people in history can forfeit the blessing of the gospel. No one people's permanent possession, it is always available to all.

To the end, Paul offered it "unhindered and with complete confidence." This summarizes the movement of the Book of Acts, from heritage to mission. The gospel would encounter obstacles; however, nothing at all could stop the gospel. Paul was bound, but the word of God was not bound.

Live the Story

You might feel that Paul played such a significant role in God's plan that you could never be like him, but Paul had only a part to play and only for his lifetime. We are each part of a story, and the model that Paul lived encourages us to play our own part in God's story.

What can you do to serve this good news of eternal life in Jesus Christ? Consider what God is calling you to do about this world's need for his love. Then, like the disciples shortly before Pentecost, ask God for the power to carry out this mission.

Leader Guide

People often view the Bible as a maze of obscure people, places, and events from centuries ago and struggle to relate it to their daily lives. IMMERSION invites us to experience the Bible as a record of God's loving revelation to humankind. These studies recognize our emotional, spiritual, and intellectual needs and welcome us into the Bible story and into deeper faith.

As leader of an IMMERSION group, you will help participants to encounter the Word of God and the God of the Word that will lead to new creation in Christ. You do not have to be an expert to lead; in fact, you will participate with your group in listening to and applying God's life-transforming Word to your lives. You and your group will explore the building blocks of the Christian faith through key stories, people, ideas, and teachings in every book of the Bible. You will also explore the bridges and points of connection between the Old and New Testaments.

Choosing and Using the Bible

The central goal of IMMERSION is engaging the members of your group with the Bible in a way that informs their minds, forms their hearts, and transforms the way they live out their Christian faith. Participants will need this study book and a Bible. IMMERSION is an excellent accompaniment to the Common English Bible (CEB). It shares with the CEB four common aims: clarity of language, faith in the Bible's power to transform lives, the emotional expectation that people will find the love of God, and the rational expectation that people will find the knowledge of God.

Other recommended study Bibles include *The New Interpreter's Study Bible* (NRSV), *The New Oxford Annotated Study Bible* (NRSV), *The HarperCollins Study Bible* (NRSV), the *NIV and TNIV Study Bibles*, and the *Archaeological Study Bible* (NIV). Encourage participants to use more than one translation. *The Message: The Bible in Contemporary Language* is a modern paraphrase of the Bible, based on the original languages. Eugene H. Peterson has created a masterful presentation of the Scripture text, which is best used alongside rather than in place of the CEB or another primary English translation.

One of the most reliable interpreters of the Bible's meaning is the Bible itself. Invite participants first of all to allow Scripture to have its say. Pay attention to context. Ask questions of the text. Read every passage with curiosity, always seeking to answer the basic Who? What? Where? When? and Why? questions.

Bible study groups should also have handy essential reference resources in case someone wants more information or needs clarification on specific words, terms, concepts, places, or people mentioned in the Bible. A Bible dictionary, Bible atlas, concordance, and one-volume Bible commentary together make for a good, basic reference library.

The Leader's Role

An effective leader prepares ahead. This leader guide provides easy to follow, step-by-step suggestions for leading a group. The key task of the leader is to guide discussion and activities that will engage heart and head and will invite faith development. Discussion questions are included, and you may want to add questions posed by you or your group. Here are suggestions for helping your group engage Scripture:

State questions clearly and simply.

Ask questions that move Bible truths from "outside" (dealing with concepts, ideas, or information about a passage) to "inside" (relating to the experiences, hopes, and dreams of the participants).

Work for variety in your questions, including compare and contrast, information recall, motivation, connections, speculation, and evaluation.

Avoid questions that call for yes-or-no responses or answers that are obvious.

Don't be afraid of silence during a discussion. It often yields especially thoughtful comments.

Test questions before using them by attempting to answer them yourself.

When leading a discussion, pay attention to the mood of your group by "listening" with your eyes as well as your ears.

Guidelines for the Group

IMMERSION is designed to promote full engagement with the Bible for the purpose of growing faith and building up Christian community. While much can be gained from individual reading, a group Bible study offers an ideal setting in which to achieve these aims. Encourage participants to bring their Bibles and read from Scripture during the session. Invite participants to consider the following guidelines as they participate in the group:

Respect differences of interpretation and understanding.

Support one another with Christian kindness, compassion, and courtesy.

Listen to others with the goal of understanding rather than agreeing or disagreeing.

Celebrate the opportunity to grow in faith through Bible study.

Approach the Bible as a dialogue partner, open to the possibility of being challenged or changed by God's Word.

Recognize that each person brings unique and valuable life experiences to the group and is an important part of the community.

Reflect theologically—that is, be attentive to three basic questions: What does this say about God? What does this say about me/us? What does this say about the relationship between God and me/us?

Commit to a *lived faith response* in light of insights you gain from the Bible. In other words, what changes in attitudes (how you believe) or actions (how you behave) are called for by God's Word?

Group Sessions

The group sessions, like the chapters themselves, are built around three sections: "Claim Your Story," "Enter the Bible Story," and "Live the Story." Sessions are designed to move participants from an awareness of their own life story, issues, needs, and experiences into an encounter and dialogue with the story of Scripture and to make decisions integrating their personal stories and the Bible's story.

The session plans in the following pages will provide questions and activities to help your group focus on the particular content of each chapter. In addition to questions and activities, the plans will include chapter title, Scripture, and faith focus.

Here are things to keep in mind for all the sessions:

Prepare Ahead

Study the Scripture, comparing different translations and perhaps a paraphrase.
Read the chapter, and consider what it says about your life and the Scripture.
Gather materials such as large sheets of paper or a markerboard with markers.
Prepare the learning area. Write the faith focus for all to see.

Welcome Participants

Invite participants to greet one another.
Tell them to find one or two people and talk about the faith focus.
Ask: What words stand out for you? Why?

Guide the Session

Look together at "Claim Your Story." Ask participants to give their reactions to the stories and examples given in each chapter. Use questions from the session plan to elicit comments based on personal experiences and insights.

Ask participants to open their Bibles and "Enter the Bible Story." For each portion of Scripture, use questions from the session plan to help participants gain insight into the text and relate it to issues in their own lives.

Step through the activity or questions posed in "Live the Story." Encourage participants to embrace what they have learned and to apply it in their daily lives.

Invite participants to offer their responses or insights about the boxed material in "Across the Testaments," "About the Scripture," and "About the Christian Faith."

Close the Session

Encourage participants to read the following week's Scripture and chapter before the next session.

Offer a closing prayer.

1. The Power of Pentecost
Acts 1–2

Faith Focus

As evidenced on the day of Pentecost, the power of the Holy Spirit enlivens Christian believers to experience and witness to the in-breaking of God's presence in the world.

Before the Session

Read Luke 1:1 and Acts 1:1. What do you see? Right. Most scholars agree that the Gospel of Luke and the Book of Acts were written by the same person, the Gospel of Luke being the first scroll mentioned in Acts 1:1. Was the writer the physician Luke who traveled with Paul? We'll leave the question up to the experts.

However, here is a suggestion: Read Acts 1–2 in several different translations. Did the reading seem slow, plodding, and difficult; or did it seem (as it does to most) as fast-moving, on-the-edge-of-your-seat, and exciting. Try to communicate this excitement as your group discusses these chapters.

Claim Your Story

Invite participants to share experiences of witnessing things so radically different that they had trouble believing them. How did these experiences change perspectives and understandings of life? In what ways did these experiences take life in entirely new directions? Participants may have trouble getting started, so have one or two of your own experiences to share to help the others begin.

Remind participants that the apostles had several such life-altering experiences in these first two chapters: Jesus' ascension and the day of Pentecost. These apostles were mostly ordinary working men, what we would call "blue-collar" today. If God could invade their lives this dramatically, what is to prevent God from entering our lives just as dramatically?

Enter the Bible Story

Invite participants to describe some of the things that had happened to the apostles from the time each was called by Jesus until the day of Pentecost. List some of these events on a markerboard or a large sheet of paper. Help participants perceive that these ordinary people had been called to share in extraordinary experiences and thereby became extraordinary themselves. What Galilean fisherman would have imagined that he would see the Messiah, experience the resurrected Christ, behold the Ascension, and preach in such a way that 3,000 persons were converted?

The Promise of Pentecost

Recall together some of Jesus' promises regarding the gift of the Spirit (see John 14, for example). Discuss: Did the apostles know what to expect as a result of these promises? Were they anticipating the Pentecost experience, or did the Pentecost experience come as an amazing surprise for them? Give reasons for answers.

Discuss: What does the apostles' Pentecost experience say to us now? What has Jesus promised us?

Preparation for Pentecost

The writer of the study material discusses several necessary preparations for the Pentecost experience. What other preparations would you add? Discuss: Can we ever be fully prepared for what God is going to do? Why or why not? If the group considers being fully prepared is unlikely, then how are we to live in anticipation of God's promises? How are we to prepare ourselves for whatever it is that God may do in our midst? Hint: How did the apostles prepare?

The Proofs and Peoples of Pentecost

Ask participants this question, writing down their ideas on a large sheet of paper or a markerboard: What visible, tangible proofs that Pentecost was of God occurred at Pentecost? Would the Pentecost experience have been as powerful without the wind and the tongues of fire; without the witnessing in different languages; and without Peter's inspired, extemporaneous sermon?

Think about the people at Pentecost. These were ordinary people gathered for a secular holiday—Jews and Gentiles. What prepared them for the Pentecost experience? (Hint to leader: Most of them were not prepared at all. God often speaks at unexpected times to unexpecting people in unexpected places.)

The Prophecy and Preaching of Pentecost

Imagine what the people who witnessed that Pentecost expected to happen next. Did the gathered Gentiles and Jews anticipate a sermon from a Galilean fisherman? Did they guess that their whole way of life would be overturned by this experience? If the answer to those two questions is no, then why were they so open to Peter's preaching, so open that 3,000 believed?

The Purpose of Pentecost

Ask each participant to say in a sentence or two the purpose of the Pentecost experience, according to Luke's account in Acts.

Live the Story

Help participants realize that Pentecost was not a one-time event, that God can and does break in upon us at times when we may least expect or realize it.

Discuss: How can we be as ready as Peter to proclaim the goodness of God when God breaks into our life experiences? However, first, how can we recognize that "breaking in" on the part of God? What might we have to be and to do to be as ready as Peter, even if our witness is just to one other person?

Invite participants to pray silently, asking for readiness to respond to God's presence through the Holy Spirit.

2. Power and Perseverance During Persecution
Acts 3–8

Faith Focus
Empowered believers stand firmly and act boldly in spite of opposition.

Before the Session
Did you discover that these chapters moved with the same immediacy of the first two chapters of the Book of Acts? The writer of Acts has a story to tell, and it is so filled with amazing details that the words tumble from his or her pen with a verve and excitement that continues to capture our imagination.

You'll want participants to experience this excitement also. Encourage them to read the Book of Acts in several translations, if possible. The Common English Bible is one excellent translation that captures the immediacy of the Book of Acts. Be sure that all participants have translations of the Bible that are easy to read and comprehend and that all are reading the assigned passages before your meetings.

Claim Your Story
One of the central themes of these chapters is people doing things they never imagined they would do and doing them in response to God's direction. Surely John and Peter never dreamed they could heal a crippled man, and Stephen may have never pictured himself as one who would wait on tables and care for the elderly. However, in response to God's call, the apostles undertook many things that they had never before imagined.

Form teams of three or four, and ask them to share personal stories of doing things they never expected to do in response to God's claim on their lives. If some participants cannot share a personal experience, encourage them to share such an experience they have heard or read.

Discuss as a whole group: What is God's promise to us when God calls us to undertake new and different things for God?

Enter the Bible Story
Healing and Preaching
Again in teams of three or four, consider this question: Peter had denied Jesus three times, and John was one of those who left Jesus and ran away from the garden of Gethsemane (Mark 14:50). What had happened to Peter and John that gave them the courage to tell the crippled man to get up and walk?

Each of us has denied Jesus and left him to run away from the dangers he faced. What happens to us that gives us the courage to attempt great things for Christ? While we may not be able to heal one who is crippled with a word as Peter and John did, what is to prevent us from witnessing for Christ as Peter did in Solomon's Portico? (Note: While scholars disagree as to just where and what Solomon's Portico was, we can assume that it was a place of importance—not the kind of place a fisherman from Galilee would usually frequent.)

Persecuted for Speaking Truth

Gather again as a whole group, and consider the persecutions faced by the apostles as they proclaimed the truth. Ask: Why were the apostles persecuted for speaking the truth? What powers or authorities are threatened when Christians speak the truth today?

Then a tough question: What is the truth? What is the simple, direct, absolute good news that any of us can share at any time, come what may? How might proclaiming Christ's love in word and action cause us to be persecuted?

(Group leader: Don't get tangled in the Ananias and Sapphira story. It demonstrates God's power; but in the context of your session, it could be a sidetrack.)

The Bicultural Witness

Conflict. In the church? Yes. Help participants perceive that any church, any congregation—even your own—is made up of human beings. Wherever there are groups of human beings, there are almost inevitably disagreements and conflicts. However, take a careful look at how the conflict in Acts 6:1-6 was solved. Ask the group to outline the steps that were used to solve the conflict. (The conflict was recognized and named. No one was blamed for the conflict. Solutions to the conflict were offered and one chosen. A division of labor and responsibility was set up, and persons accepted their tasks and eagerly fulfilled them.) Then talk about the extent to which that model of conflict resolution happens in churches today and in your church.

Stephen, one of those with new responsibilities, was "set up" by the enemies of the Christ movement. Consider what Stephen did not do: He did not claim to be a simple table waiter who knew nothing, an action that may have saved his life. Then consider what he did: He proclaimed Christ's love not in judgment toward others, but as God's gift for all.

Ask: What do we do when we are opposed or ridiculed by those forces (or people) seemingly at odds with the Christian faith? What can Stephen's example teach us about how to be bold without being confrontational in our faith?

Live the Story

Ask each person in the group to reflect silently on the characters in these chapters—Peter and John, Ananias and Sapphira, Stephen, the deacons, and others. Ask each person to write down on a piece of paper—for his or her eyes only!—the character with which he or she can most identify. Then ask each participant to pray in silence for the courage to proclaim the gospel truth, the good news of salvation, regardless of the cost, in spite of what opposition may come, and no matter what others might think.

3. God's Spirit Compels the Church Across Cultural Boundaries
Acts 8–11

Faith Focus

The Holy Spirit knows no boundaries, freely offering the gift of faith in Christ to all who accept it and calling believers to bear witness to that gift.

Before the Session

Now striding onto the stage is one of the most colorful yet enigmatic characters in the Scripture: Saul (Paul) of Tarsus. Originally intent on wiping out all followers of Jesus, Paul became the great champion of Christianity and devoted his life and death to proclaiming salvation through Jesus the Christ.

Jesus' life and ministry is bracketed by two men who were at once radically alike and radically different. Before Jesus began his ministry, John the Baptist, the wild desert prophet proclaimed a gospel of readiness for the coming Lord. Unkempt, unlettered, untamed, John emerged from the desert to prepare the way for the Lord. After Jesus' ascension, Paul, the wild persecutor of the Way, found himself radically transformed into the great missionary and evangelist for the very Way he had sought to destroy.

Paul: sophisticated, urbane, highly educated, yet totally committed to his Lord and Savior. John the Baptist: rustic, solitary, highly passionate, yet totally committed to preparing the way for the Lord. Given these two examples, what kinds of people does God call to do God's will? Every kind, including each one of us!

Claim Your Story

Ask participants to settle themselves comfortably, to listen as you read a list of statements and questions, and to ponder their responses to each of the questions silently and prayerfully.

Here are the statements and questions. Pause after each one to allow participants to reflect.

- Have you always believed wholeheartedly in Jesus as the Christ? Recall a time when your faith was wavering and uncertain, when your doubt was great.
- What did God do to get you back on track? Think of persons or events that may have helped you turn back to God.
- What has God asked of you at various times in your life? How did you respond? Did you argue with God before responding? What were some of your arguments? (For example, "I'm not good enough" or "I'm too busy.")

• If God asked you today to witness for Christ in a particular way with a particular group of persons, what would be your response? How would you know that it was God who was calling you?

Do not ask for anyone to share thoughts or feelings in response to these questions and statements. However, if someone indicates a need to contribute, let her or him do so.

Enter the Bible Story
Philip in Samaria and With the African Official

The writer of the study book indicates that the stories of Philip in Samaria and with the Ethiopian official are vivid testimony of the universality of God's redemption of all humankind. We can only imagine how strange Philip's words must have sounded in Samaria and to the Ethiopian, but his testimony was so powerful that conversions took place. Stranger still, though, was a Jew befriending Samaritans and Gentiles, both considered unclean by strict Jewish laws.

Ask: Who in our day and age would be as radically different from us as the Samaritans and the Ethiopians were to Philip? Atheists? Muslims? Hindus? How do you think God calls us in our day to share the love of Christ with people and people groups different from us?

Calling Saul to the Gentiles

While the story of Paul's conversion and Ananias's visit to Paul is well known, we seldom get to the emotional level when we consider this event.

Discuss: What was going through Paul's heart and soul as he began to believe in Jesus as the Christ? Regret? shame? guilt? something else? How do you think Paul dealt with the emotional upheaval of his conversion?

What was going through Ananias's mind and heart as he headed to the place his enemy Paul was residing in order to tell him of God's love? What was going through the heart and soul of each of these men when Ananias said, "Brother Saul"? Could you go to your greatest enemy and call him or her brother or sister? Why or why not?

Converting Cornelius, Converting the Church

Some people just don't get it. Peter was like that. A Jewish man of the Law, Peter had trouble believing that God's love extended to the Gentiles, so God showed Peter the facts in an eloquent way.

Ask: If God let down that sheet before you today and said, "These are my beloved children," who would be there? Who might you be most surprised to see?

Live the Story

Give each person in your group an index card or piece of cardstock. Invite participants to print on it the name of a person they would call an enemy—in particular, an enemy to the Christian faith. Ask them to keep that name in a pocket, a wallet, or a purse, and to pray for that person, in anticipation of when they find the courage or the opportunity to share with that person the love of Christ.

Close the session with a prayer of gratitude for the free gift of faith and for the opportunity to live the faith so that others might come to Christ.

4. Peter, Paul, and Barnabas on the Road
Acts 12–15

Faith Focus

A personal encounter with the living Jesus redirects one's life and propels it into service of God, work that is hard and hopeful.

Before the Session

The Book of Acts now moves into a long section detailing Paul's missionary journeys. so reading with a map alongside will be helpful. Look in the back of your Bible, in a Bible dictionary, or at any one of several excellent Bible atlases for maps outlining Paul's extensive travels.

If you have access to a large map of the Mediterranean world at the time of Paul, consider posting it in your meeting room, using brightly colored sticky notes to mark the various places Paul witnessed for the Lord.

Claim Your Story

What is right, and what is wrong? Broach this subject by asking participants why they are members of your particular denomination and not members of another denomination. Some participants might indicate that the reason lies in "liking the way we do things" and "not liking the way 'they' do things."

Multiply this attitude many times over, and you know what was facing the early church. They, too, asked what is right and what is wrong; and even after much discussion and prayer, they often still could not agree.

However, what they did agree on was the centrality of Jesus Christ, God's gift of salvation for . . . what? That was part of the problem. Was God's gift of salvation for the Jewish Christians only? for the Gentile Christians only? for both? Think of our times. Is salvation only for Christians of our denomination? only for Christians who do the same things we do and condemn the same things we disdain? Or is it for all, which may mean even those whose lifestyles we find repugnant? The early church's experience is 2,000 years old and yet as contemporary as tomorrow.

Enter the Bible Story

Danger for God's work

Imprisonment. Assassination. Constant threats. These greeted the earliest followers of the Way. We're not faced with these kinds of hardships, but what are the dangers inherent in our claim of Jesus Christ as Lord? If our faith is never put to the test, what might happen to our faith in God? To what extent do you think our own faith is made deeper by testing, especially by testing from outside?

Encourage participants to give reasons and examples for responding as they do.

Leaving Comfort for God's Work

Ask: Who authorized Paul for his missionary endeavors? The early church did nothing without a sense that the Holy Spirit was authorizing all their activities. How are persons called today to leave the comfort of the familiar and take up the mantle of service for Christ? How can a person be sure that he or she is being summoned by the Holy Spirit and not by some selfish interest or misguided intent?

Read Acts 13:1-4 carefully. Paul may not have intended to be a missionary; it was at the prodding of the Holy Spirit and the "ordination" by the community of believers that propelled Paul to travel throughout the world. Explore the idea that God might be calling individual members of your group, or the whole group, toward a particular mission endeavor. Where are the mission fields in your community?

Notice how successfully Paul and Barnabas began their work. Success with the proconsul in the conflict with Elymas, success (at the beginning) in Antioch of Pisidia, and even success in turning toward the Gentiles after being rejected by the Jews in Antioch. What might this say to persons today who feel called by the Holy Spirit to take a stand for God? God does not promise unlimited success but does promise to be with those God calls. Paul's experience of being stoned at Lystra is testimony to this.

Ask participants to share their experiences of stepping out for God and discovering success, then encountering difficulties but finding reassurance that God was with them.

Struggles Even Among God's People

The Jerusalem Conference recounted in Acts 15 testifies that God's ways are far beyond the ways of human beings. The Jewish believers in Christ felt that to become a Christian, one must first become a Jew. The Jerusalem Conference resolved this but not without disagreement.

Ask participants to reflect on the rules that some groups hold that may impede others from knowing Christ fully. For example, some denominations insist that the sacraments be performed in certain ways, others hold that all must subscribe to a particular confession of faith, and still others may require that worship be conducted in a specific manner. Ask this question (but invite participants to reflect before they answer): Does our congregation require anything of members that may exclude some from our fellowship?

Live the Story

Ask participants to highlight the main points of these chapters in Acts. They should indentify the leading of the Holy Spirit, the opportunity to spread the Gospel, and the radical inclusiveness of the kingdom of God. Ask: Given what we have learned in these chapters of Acts, to what areas of mission or service are we as Christ's followers today called? Are we more encouraged by the hope inherent in such work or more fearful because of the difficulties that may hinder such work?

Something to explore as a group in following up on this study are ways you might "hit the road," so to speak, as a team of missionaries, looking for places outside the walls of the church to take the love of Christ (for example, disaster relief, inner-city ministry, prison inmate mentoring, advocacy for the poor and marginalized, new church planting). Pray for God's guidance and strength as you identify ways to serve God and neighbor, even when serving may be difficult.

5. New Possibilities and New Perils for Paul
Acts 16–18

Faith Focus
The work of God in the world involves believers in cooperative and inclusive partnerships that lead to radical demonstrations of faithful discipleship.

Before the Session
On a large map of the Mediterranean region, mark the route Paul took in these three chapters. Highlight the several cities in which he preached, was imprisoned, and was persecuted. Post this map in your meeting room, and make reference to it throughout this session. Roughly estimate some of the distances Paul traveled in these chapters. For example, his journey from Troas to Neapolis was about 150 miles.

What town, city, or area is about 150 miles from your church? Couching the distances of Paul's travels in terms of your own geographic area will help participants understand the scope of Paul's journeys. However, he traveled by walking (about three miles per hour) or by boat (about four miles per hour, depending on the winds).

Claim Your Story
Ask: Has Christ ever turned the world upside down for you? If so, when and how? Help the group to understand that few of us can recall exact dates or specific places in which we suddenly comprehended God's love through Christ in such a way that it prompted radical change. For many of us, perhaps most of us, this "turning of the world upside down" was more gradual, a growing awareness that a commitment to Christ changes one's life in many ways.

Talk about how commitment to Christ alters many things about who we are, what we do, and how we view others. Such commitment certainly changed Paul. These three chapters of Acts describe Paul traveling widely among Gentiles, a group of persons with whom he would have had no association at all prior to his conversion. Where have you seen evidence (in yourself or in another) of a profound change in attitude, behavior, or purpose, caused by an encounter with Christ?

Enter the Bible Story
Finding Partners for Mission and Struggling With Guidance
What does Paul do in Acts 16:3? Is he compromising, accommodating to others' wishes by having Timothy circumcised? Paul wanted Timothy to be perceived as a Jew because Paul was going to be preaching in synagogues. Was Paul "backsliding" here, or was he able to determine when and how to compromise and accommodate for the sake

of the gospel? What does this passage suggest to us about compromising and accommodating for the sake of the gospel? How can we be sure that our compromises are for the gospel's sake and not just for our own ease and comfort? In what areas might we compromise and in what areas of faith must we never compromise, no matter what?

Consider a related question based on this same short passage of Scripture (Acts 16:9): How can you and I be sure that it is God directing us and not our own wishes and desires? To what extent do you think God still gives guidance through visions? Participants might want to share experiences related to feeling led by God.

Persecuted for Spiritual Liberation and the Missionaries' Own Liberation

Recall together how work of liberation is accomplished in Acts 16. First, Paul liberated the slave girl. Second, Paul and Silas were liberated by the power of God. Third, the jailer and his family were liberated by Paul's witness for Christ. Demonstrate how these three steps illustrate an expanding cycle: As we seek to liberate others, we discover that we ourselves are liberated; and that in turn allows us to liberate others even more.

Ask: Liberated *from* what and liberated *for* what in each of these steps? Invite participants to encapsulate this idea in brief sentences, such as: "As we forgive, we are forgiven." "As we love, so are we loved and enabled to love even more."

The Missionaries in Athens and in Corinth

Paul was not always successful in his efforts to share the gospel. He preached powerfully in Athens but was met with skepticism. Check Paul's experience in Athens and in Corinth. Do you suppose Paul was discouraged and disappointed? Discuss: What transpired in Corinth that gave Paul the courage to press on? What does Paul's experience in Corinth say to us and to our efforts to proclaim the gospel of Jesus Christ?

Live the Story

Close this session with a bidding prayer. Ask participants to pray in silence in response to these phrases that you read aloud. Pause for at least a minute following each phrase. Here are the phrases:

Lord, these are the people I know who need to be liberated . . .

Lord, in these areas of my life I need to be liberated . . .

Lord, I get discouraged when I try to proclaim the gospel . . .

Lord, I seek your direction in my life in these ways . . .

Lord, I am willing to witness for you no matter the cost . . .

Conclude by inviting the group to join in praying the Lord's Prayer.

6. Paul in Ephesus: The Gospel and the Greeks
Acts 19–20

Faith Focus
Proclaiming the good news of God's grace has the disruptive power to change people and their culture.

Before the Session
Because of the significance of Ephesus in the life and ministry of Paul, research the ancient city of Ephesus. Check a good Bible dictionary or a detailed commentary for information about this important city. Some Bible atlases will also provide background on major cities such as Ephesus. What city in the United States might seem today most like the Ephesus of Paul's time?

Claim Your Story
"Just when everything was going so well, things started to fall apart!"

Begin by asking participants to relate an experience similiar to Paul's at Ephesus. Things were going so well. Paul was being received well in the synagogue and in the lecture hall. People were joining the Way. Then everything went wrong. When has that happened to you?

Then ask participants to relate experiences (or imagine what one might look like today) in which doing the right thing had a negative impact on someone else's financial position. Like the case of the Ephesian silversmiths, who saw their livelihood threatened, when does the Christian church take stances that threaten the livelihoods of others (people, groups, institutions)? Ask for specific examples, and encourage discussion.

Enter the Bible Story
Finding Culturally Relevant Teaching Venues and Threatening Local Religious Exploitation
Recall with the group that Paul almost always commenced his preaching in a new location in the local synagogue. Why do you think Paul did that? (Some reasons: Paul was most at home in a synagogue; those in the synagogue were open to a deeper understanding of the will of God; those in the synagogue knew the one true God; Paul did not need to "convert" them from polytheism to monotheism before he could talk about Christ.) When Paul did not gain a hearing in the synagogue, where did he go next? While Acts speaks of Paul preaching in synagogues and lecture halls, the story of Paul in Athens indicates that Paul was eager to preach wherever people were. Explore insights in that fact for Christians today.

Read aloud Demetrius's speech to the silversmiths in Acts 19:25b-27. Afterward, as a group, discuss Demetrius's dialogue. What was his primary concern? What was his secondary concern? Demetrius seems to have been motivated more by the threat to his business than he was to honoring the goddess Artemis, yet he tried to hide his economic concerns behind a veil of religious concern. Where do you see evidence of such situations today? When do people become "religious" because it pays? Encourage the group to give reasons and examples.

One of the frightening dimensions of this story is that Demetrius managed to stir up a riot, prompting mob rule to supplant reason and rationality. We have only to recall the Civil Rights struggles and the Viet Nam War protests to see how quickly and easily a group of citizens can be transformed, for good or for ill, into an irrational mob. Invite participants to relate experiences in which they witnessed gatherings of people becoming uncontrollable mobs.

What happened at Ephesus? The voice of one individual, the town clerk, quieted the mob, a mob that was ready to stone Paul and the other Christians to death. Did God choose and use this town clerk? Did this town clerk act in his own selfish interest? Did the town clerk have anything to gain—financially or in any other way—by rescuing Paul? What insights come from this story of Paul at Ephesus?

Suspense Builds en Route to Jerusalem

The enemies of Paul increase in numbers and boldness. They wanted to do away with Paul as he was a threat not only to their financial security but to their very way of life. Paul made good his escape from Ephesus and its surroundings, but he longed to leave those who lived in Ephesus and who believed in Christ with a final word, thus the meeting with the elders from Ephesus at Miletus.

Read aloud Paul's message to the Ephesian elders (Acts 20:18b-35), asking participants to listen closely to the words. Then invite each person to summarize Paul's farewell address in a single sentence. As time allows, share these single sentences around the group.

Live the Story

Few Christians in the United States are called to "live the story" quite like Paul, that is, to face an angry mob intent on destruction. However, almost every Christians has been or will be called upon to stand up for Christ in the face of cultural opposition. Talk for a few minutes about the various ways contemporary culture opposes the message and the mission of the gospel.

Who are the Ephesian silversmiths of today that most challenge your faith? How can you take the example of Paul in Acts 19–20 to gain the courage to face that kind of challenge? How do you understand the "disruptive power" of God's Holy Spirit and the role of the church in our society? Where might you see yourself being a channel for the disruptive Holy Spirit?

Ask the group to offer sentence prayers for courage, faith, and power.

7. Paul on the Defense
Acts 21–24

Faith Focus
Captivity to the gospel of Jesus Christ frees us from the confines of religion and of society in order to proclaim that all are invited to belong to God's family.

Before the Session
In preparation for this session, consult a good Bible dictionary to learn the identities and roles of several of the persons mentioned in these chapters. You will want to learn about centurions and tribunes and the significance of persons such as Felix, Tertullus, Drusilla, and two men named Ananias. While Paul remains the primary character in Acts, these "bit players" illuminate the ways God was working through the former persecutor of the Christians.

Notice, too, how Paul's involvement with people had spiraled up from contact with ordinary persons to contact with the highest levels of government.

Claim Your Story
Part of this story of Paul's continuing evangelization of the world is Paul's entanglement with the governmental bureaucracy of the day. Who among us cannot relate at least one story of getting caught up in governmental "red tape"? Finding our way through the maze of the legislative process, at the local or the national level, seems exhaustive at times; and yet Paul had to negotiate this same maze, often with a price on his head. However, Paul could not leave his calling any more than we can turn our backs on what God compels us to do for the sake of the gospel. When has the bureaucracy of government become a hindrance or a nuisance for you in being a Christian?

Enter the Bible Story
Beaten for False Accusation
Paul had been raised as a deeply religious Jew; consequently, Jerusalem was the most holy of cities for him. He longed to be in contact with the apostles who were still in the Jerusalem area. He was not returning as a conquering hero, despite his successes; he was returning as one eager to learn more about his Lord, Christ Jesus, from some of those who had walked with Jesus before and after his resurrection.

Reflect briefly as a group on the importance of "place" in our lives. Invite the group to recall the homes where they were raised; a church building and neighborhood that was especially meaningful during their early years; a place, perhaps a church camp, where they first began to internalize the reality of Christ. Jerusalem had this kind of tug on Paul, and he always wanted to return there. Given the significance of place for Paul and for us, discuss what may have been Paul's feelings as he was dragged from the Temple and beaten almost fatally in this city close to his heart. How might we feel and react if we went "home" and were treated with contempt and physical abuse?

Paul defended himself before the mob by retelling the story of his conversion. Under great duress, Paul told of all that God had done for him through Christ. Seldom must we do so under duress. So why do we often find telling others what Christ has done for us difficult to do?

Eluding Assassins

Paul's escape from those who had pledged to kill him is an interesting "side" story. Quickly retell the story for the whole group. Ask: What does this story mean for us today? Can we always rely on God to save us in difficult situations? Give reasons and examples for answers. Does God rescue us the way we expect or want to be rescued, or does God rescue us in ways we never expected? Encourage participants to explain their responses.

Accused Before the Governor

Paul had parlayed his Roman citizenship into a chance to state his case before the highest authorities. Why do you think Paul chose to continue his case to this level? Would his life not have been easier if he had agreed to remain silent? What criteria do we use to determine how far and how tenaciously we are to proclaim the gospel?

Live the Story

Paul's story in these chapters is a story of determination to proclaim the gospel no matter what—no matter the threat he felt from fellow Jews (with religious agendas), and no matter the danger posed by Roman officials (with political agendas). Like Paul, standing for a God who loves everyone can sometimes bring us into conflict with those who bend faith to serve their own agendas and with those who see Christian faith as a threat to the political establishment.

When have you come into conflict over who can belong in the circle of God's family? or in the fellowship of your congregation? When have you witnessed or heard a person of faith (yourself even) promoting her own theological agenda at the expense of another's? When have you caught yourself being unable to accept another's experience of God because it was so different from your own?

Consider the tricky relationship between politics and religion in our culture. To what extent do we experience the interference or hindrance of government in our life of faith?

Invite your group to be alert during the coming week for news articles about conflict involving the church and its witness in our world, perhaps one where religious and political agendas are in contention with each other. Pray for that situation, and pray for how you might respond to it.

8. The Gospel Reaches Rome
Acts 25–28

Faith Focus

Christian believers boldly confront the power structures of the world, confident in the gospel's power to accomplish God's purposes.

Before the Session

A good Bible dictionary will give you information about some of the key players in these chapters, such as Festus and Agrippa.

Ask participants to write a paragraph describing Paul as they have come to know him through Acts. Encourage them to keep this paragraph but not to refer to it again until they have studied Paul's letters. Then invite them to look at their paragraph and compare their image of Paul from Acts with their understanding of Paul from his letters.

Claim Your Story

Share with participants the two main thrusts of these chapters: Paul's defense before the highest political authorities and Paul's perilous journey to Rome. Some speculate that Paul knew he could spread the gospel even more widely if he went to Rome. Others believe that Paul appealed to save his life in order to continue to proclaim the gospel.

What else might have motivated his appeal? Put yourself in Paul's shoes: Would you have appealed to Caesar? Why or why not? Why do you think Paul appealed to Caesar? If you were asked to share your testimony about what Christ has done in your life with the governor of your state, would your witness before powerful persons be the same or different from your witness to a friend or relative? Encourage participants to give reasons for their answer.

Enter the Bible Story
An Apostle's Appeal and a Governor's Consultation

Paul had been imprisoned for two years, although Felix often sent for Paul and talked with him during Paul's imprisonment. What kinds of things do you think were going through Paul's mind during these years?

Once the new authority took over for the retiring one, the new authority did not have a history with Paul the prisoner. Thus, Festus sought to try Paul on fabricated charges; and Paul reacted by demanding a trial—not in Jerusalem, where the jury would be "stacked" against him, but in Rome itself. Discuss Paul's actions. Were they careful, calculated, and foolhardy; or were they the least negative of several options? Discuss Paul's appeal to the emperor. What part might the Holy Spirit have played in his decision?

Paul's Defense of the Good News

An audience before the king! How do you think Paul prepared for this event? Had you been Paul, how would you have prepared? Have you ever had to appear before government authorities? How did you prepare or wish you had prepared? Paul relied on the story of his conversion as the impetus of his preaching. Why are we often reluctant to tell the story of our relationship with Christ as the stimulus for our witnessing? On what occasions might our faith stories be precisely the right entry point for sharing the gospel with others?

Risks at Sea

Have you ever had to travel somewhere, and you didn't know if you wanted to get there or didn't want to get there? Paul may have had the same feelings on that dangerous boat trip to Rome. Sailing on the Mediterranean was in its infancy at the time; shipwrecks were commonplace, and arrival at one's destination "in one piece" was rare.

Notice a couple of details about the journey. Paul continued to witness for his faith in Christ wherever he was and despite any hardship, and he was passionately concerned about the safety of the others on board. What does this say about Paul? What does this say about how we express our faith in moments of crisis? Invite people to share occasions where they (or others) were able to maintain a Christian witness in spite of circumstances that could have easily provoked an unchristian response.

Reasoning in Rome

It is hard to imagine that Paul's sojourn in Rome was what he expected. Essentially, he was under house arrest, though free to proclaim the gospel. What does this closing situation say about Paul? What does this final chapter say about Luke's purpose in Acts?

Live the Story

As the study book writer observes, the phrase "unhindered and with complete confidence" aptly summarizes "the movement of the Book of Acts, from heritage to mission. The gospel would encounter obstacles. However, nothing at all could stop the gospel."

Invite each participant to reflect a few moments on the Book of Acts they have read over the last few weeks. Then ask everyone to write a brief paragraph describing how coming to know Paul through the Book of Acts has affected his or her faith. Have them consider the extent to which Paul's story encouraged them in making a stronger witness for Christ in their lives.

Before closing, invite those who are willing to share their paragraphs aloud. Then conclude the sharing time by reading aloud, in unison, part of Paul's salutation in Philippians 1:1-7.

CPSIA information can be obtained at www.ICGtesting.com
Printed in the USA
LVOW10s0005030516

486372LV00003B/4/P